Twentieth-Century British Poetry

Twentieth-Century British Poetry
A Critical Introduction

John Williams
Senior Lecturer in English, Thames Polytechnic

© John Williams 1987

First published in Great Britain 1987 by
Edward Arnold (Publishers) Ltd, 41 Bedford Square, London WC1B 3DQ

Edward Arnold (Australia) Pty Ltd, 80 Waverley Road, Caulfield East,
  Victoria 3145, Australia

Edward Arnold, 3 East Read Street, Baltimore, Maryland 21202, USA

British Library Cataloguing in Publication Data

Williams, John *1946–*
   Twentieth century British poetry: a
critical introduction.
   1. English poetry—20th century—
History and criticism
   I. Title
   821'.912'09   PR601

ISBN 0-7131-6499-9

All rights reserved. No part of this publication may be reproduced, stored in a retrieval system, or transmitted in any form or by any means, electronic, photocopying, recording, or otherwise, without the prior permission of Edward Arnold (Publishers) Ltd.

Text set in 10/11 pt Plantin Compugraphic
by Colset Private Limited, Singapore
Made and printed in Great Britain
by Richard Clay Ltd., Bungay, Suffolk

Contents

Preface	vii
Acknowledgements	x
1 The Romantic Heritage	1
2 Modernism 1900–1930	17
3 Post-Modernist Poetry 1930–1950	41
4 Poetry since 1945	70
Conclusion	103
Bibliography	107
Index of poets cited	111
General Index	115

for Rebecca

Preface

This book offers a critical introductory study of British poetry from 1900 to the present day. While it is intended as a guide for those encountering the period for the first time, readers already familiar with the general outline of ideas that have fashioned the evolution of poetry during this period, and with the poetry itself, are invited to re-examine a number of critical assumptions that have developed, particularly in the light of the way the Romantic Movement of the previous century may be understood to have influenced twentieth-century poetry. An important part of the discussion therefore is concerned with the theoretical debate, from the consequences of Matthew Arnold's influential critique of Romanticism in the second half of the nineteenth century, through to the often controversial contemporary debate on literary theory, and the function of criticism.

Any book which aims to be both an introduction, and relatively brief, inevitably creates a problem of coverage. Studies in contemporary British poetry have tended recently to embark at 1945. The decision here to look at the whole century is important in so far as it makes possible a detailed assessment of crucial pre-1945 influences on subsequent work; but equally it intensifies the problem of deciding what, and what not, to include. The danger is that such a book becomes little more than an annotated list, or, in order to do justice to individual poets and poems, the choice becomes so selective as to lose sight of any overall picture.

In the present case, though omissions have inevitably and regrettably been necessary, the recognized canon of 'important' or 'influential' work finds its place alongside some less predictable poetry that may at least stimulate discussion and reappraisal. The need for close textual readings rather than purely descriptive accounts has certainly not been abandoned, and the intention here is both to help and encourage those using this book primarily in its introductory capacity, and to engage the well prepared reader with key issues in the texts themselves.

The main rationale for selection from a period in which so much poetry has been written, and in which so much has been written about poetry, stems from the initial Modernist critique of Romanticism in the early twentieth century, and the subsequent reappraisal of the Romantic Movement which coincided with the influence of Surrealism in Britain between the wars. The complexity of the Romantic Movement itself presents a problem in this respect, and the first chapter is designed partly to show just how variable a commodity nineteenth-century Romanticism became. The fact remains that throughout this century, important literary movements and trends have defined themselves often with a very specific sense of reference to Romanticism.

The latter part of Chapter 1 considers this situation with reference to W.B. Yeats and the Symbolist Movement, and to Thomas Hardy's response to nineteenth-century Romanticism. The theme is continued in Chapter 2 through a reading of Imagist and Modernist poetry, indicating the significance of T.E. Hulme's and Ezra Pound's unequivocal condemnation of the Romantic Movement for a full understanding of Modernism as it established itself primarily through the poetry and criticism of T.S. Eliot. Equally important here is the influence of the First World War, and its major poets.

In Chapter 3, the Marxist poetry of the Auden group in the 1930s, arguably containing elements of a Romantic reaction to Modernism, is considered alongside the 'neo-Romanticism' of the same period, which was profoundly antagonistic to the Auden group, and which reached its climax with the outbreak of war in 1939.

After the war, the work of poets who became identified with what in the mid 50s had become known as The Movement, in many ways typified the general trend of post-war British poetry. Movement poetry subsequently became increasingly associated (much to his dislike) with the work in particular of Philip Larkin, and represents a critical reaction against a pre-war theory and practice of poetry characterized by Romantic/Surrealist excess. The final chapter considers some of the major responses to Movement poetry, many of which imply the need for a rediscovery of elements of imaginative perception that had first begun to appear in a form accessible to the contemporary reader in the Romantic Movement of the late eighteenth and early nineteenth century. The recourse which many major post-war British poets have had to the poetry and criticism of that period, notably Ted Hughes and Seamus Heaney, indicates the perpetuation of a debate which has informed British poetry for the last 200 years, and, given the inevitable shifts in context and emphasis, seems destined to continue for a long time to come.

A Note on Texts

Details of poems and secondary sources given in footnotes refer where possible to readily available editions. Footnotes also indicate abbreviated versions to be used subsequently within the text. The abbreviations are also indexed to facilitate finding full details in the relevant footnote. A brief bibliography of the main anthologies used, and of further secondary texts will be found at the end of the book. As an additional aid to reference, there is a separate index of poets referred to, which incorporates also reference to the poems discussed.

Preface

Acknowledgements

The responsibility for whatever errors this book may include is of course wholly mine, but I would like to thank the following for attempting to help me keep those errors to a minimum: firstly the publishers, whose help and advice have been invaluable; numerous friends and colleagues who were prepared to discuss issues and give advice on texts and sources; I owe a particular debt of gratitude to the 'Auden class' of 1986 at Thames Polytechnic for a series of formal and informal discussions which were a source of great help as well as enjoyment; and last but not least, I am indebted to my wife for putting up with me during the protracted birth-pangs occasioned by the writing of this book, while she herself was far more patiently preparing to give birth to our daughter.

Acknowledgements

The publishers would like to thank the following for their permission to include poems:

Carcanet Press Limited and New Directions Publishing Corporation for Hilda Doolittle's 'Oread' from *Collected Poems 1911-1944* copyright © 1984 by the Estate of Hilda Doolittle, reprinted by permission; Andre Deutsch for the first of Geoffrey Hill's *The Mercian Hymns*; Faber and Faber Limited for Philip Larkin's 'Days' from *The Whitsun Weddings*; David Higham Associates Limited for part of Dylan Thomas's 'And Death Shall Have no Dominion' from *Collected Poems*; John Murray for part of John Betjeman's 'Aldershot Crematorium' from *Collected Poems*; Oxford University Press for part of Charles Tomlinson's 'How Still the Hawk' from *Collected Poems*; George Sassoon for Siegfried Sassoon's 'Suicide in the Trenches' from *Collected Poems 1908-56* and A.P. Watt for W.B. Yeats's 'The Rose of the World' from *The Collected Poems of W.B. Yeats*.

1
The Romantic Heritage

The starting point for most discussions of English literature in the twentieth century is to agree with the historian's verdict that the early 1900s was a period of crisis. The precise nature and seriousness of that crisis – both politically and in the arts – remains a matter for debate. The purpose of the first chapter of this book is to prepare the ground for a consideration of Modernism in British poetry between 1900 and 1930. Fully to understand Modernism, we need to look at both the literary and social contexts of the crisis to which poets of that period were consciously responding. For our contextual understanding to be of any real use it is necessary – however briefly – to refer back to the sense of crisis registered by poets in the late eighteenth and early nineteenth centuries, and to take account of the way they responded then.

It has been argued that the first two decades of the twentieth century, the latter dominated by the impact of the First World War, saw the final demise of an ideal of cultural and social order established as far back as the sixteenth century, an ideal rooted in an agrarian, rural concept of social stability, and more often than not expressed in a cultural language which reserved its highest regard for Classical art forms associated with ancient Greece and Rome.[1] At no time was the Classical model a more dominant feature in English literature than during the eighteenth century, the so-called Augustan period, when imitations and translations of Juvenal, Horace and Virgil abounded, and virtually every poet who aspired to greatness planned epic works in the manner of John Milton's *Paradise Lost* (1667), itself modelled on the blank verse of the fifteenth-century Italian poet, Tasso.

The late eighteenth and early nineteenth centuries saw the emergence in England of the Romantic Movement, challenging in part at least the hegemony of eighteenth-century Augustan Classicism, and where not aggressively challenging, certainly registering a sense of profound uncertainty. It was impossible to avoid the conclusion that the established literary models seemed inadequate to the poet's needs, a development

---

[1] V. de S. Pinto, *Crisis In English Poetry*, London: Hutchinson (1967) pp. 99–100. Hereafter *Pinto*.

inevitably linked to the fact that new and far-reaching debates were surfacing with regard to the political ordering of society. The literary crisis associated in the first instance with the poetry of William Blake, but also identified in the work of so-called 'late Augustans' like Oliver Goldsmith, Thomas Gray and George Crabbe, and subsequently with William Wordsworth in the 1790s and early 1800s, is generally closely identified with the political events of the period which came to have their focal point in the French Revolution.

The literary crisis of the early twentieth century expressed itself in many respects as a response to the initial impact of the Romantic Movement on English literature, and to the way Romanticism had subsequently influenced literary evolution. M.H. Abrams has suggested that Romanticism is for the most part little more than 'a convenient fiction for the historian',[2] and it is important to realize at the outset that we are not looking at a coherently classifiable body of literature. Blake certainly expressed considerable hostility towards art founded on Classical principles, and championed the northern European tradition of 'Gothic' form which he understood as encouraging far more the free play of imaginative ideas and individual genius. This was by no means wholly characteristic of the views of other major Romantic poets, however; Wordsworth was a life-long admirer of Alexander Pope (1688–1744), a major figure in the Augustan Classical tradition of the early eighteenth century, while Shelley's commitment to the study of Classical philosophy and literature, notably Plato and Aeschylus, influenced much – if not all – of his work.

Just what the Romantic Movement was, and more importantly, what it had meant for literature (especially in the realm of poetry), provided the subject for a debate that in due course became profoundly influential in shaping the nature of Modernist poetry after 1900. In the mid nineteenth century, Matthew Arnold's critique of the Romantic Movement stressed the intimate relationship between 'English poetry of the first quarter of this century' and 'the immense stir of the French Revolution'. Arnold's central thesis was that involvement with the 'political, practical character' of Revolutionary politics diverted Byron, Shelley and Wordsworth from the intellectual pursuits they required to produce truly great work: 'This makes Byron so empty of matter, Shelley so incoherent, Wordsworth, even, profound as he is, yet so wanting in completeness and variety.'[3] The fault lies not so much with the poets themselves, however, as with the society that nurtured them; a society immersed in ideas engendered by the French Revolution would not have a 'national glow of life and thought . . . as in the Athens of Pericles, or the England of Elizabeth. That was the poet's

---

[2]M.H. Abrams, *The Mirror and the Lamp*, Oxford: Oxford University Press (1953) p. 100. Hereafter *Abrams*.
[3]Matthew Arnold, *Essays in Criticism* (1865), 'The Function of Criticism at the Present Time', in *Selected Prose*, ed. P.J. Keating, Penguin Books (1970). Quotations above p. 136 and pp. 134–5. Hereafter *Arnold*.

weakness' (*Arnold* p. 135). The creative impulses of Byron and Wordsworth 'had their source in a great movement of feeling, not in a great movement of mind' (*Arnold* p. 136). 'Feeling' implied a development of individualism; 'a great movement of mind', on the other hand, suggests a collective consciousness on the part of society of which the poet becomes the mouthpiece. This distinction must be clear if we are to understand the twentieth-century Modernist critique of Romanticism put forward by T.S. Eliot.

Arnold was drawing attention to the quality for which Romanticism is best known, an emphasis on emotion and a free play of imagination; what he found distasteful in this was the extent to which it indicated a degree of anti-intellectualism on the part of the Romantics; thus his complaint that 'Wordsworth cared little for books' (*Arnold* p. 135).

What prompted poets at the turn of the eighteenth century to explore what Wordsworth himself called 'the essential passions of the heart'[4] to the extent they did, was a sense of dissociation from society that was already becoming evident in the work of many late Augustan poets. Both Goldsmith (in *The Deserted Village*, 1770) and Gray (in the *Elegy in a Country Churchyard*, 1750) portray themselves as poets who are victims of the decay of a rural social order. Goldsmith's lament is two-fold: firstly, for the depopulation of the countryside, and the increasing, morally unhealthy attractions of city life, and secondly for the fact that this leaves him with no 'public' for his poetry. In the past, the work of poets was understood to have been intimately bound up with every aspect of society, a conviction that assumed society – regardless of its recognized inequalities of degree – to be ultimately an organically whole body. Here lay the attraction that the Augustan poets of the Roman Empire had for an eighteenth-century Classical, 'Augustan' poet like Samuel Johnson. Blake was one of the first poets of the period to insist that, given the way English society was changing (like ancient Rome, its acquisitive, materialistic era of Empire building was drawing to a justly fraught close) the Augustan model appeared increasingly decadent and anachronistic. The divisions within society between rich and poor, between those who had a stake in the political nation and the many who did not, were of a harmfully destructive order.

Wordworth's diagnosis, expressed in his 'Preface' to the 1800 edition of *Lyrical Ballads*, was that Augustan poetic form, admirable in its inception, had degenerated into a poetic language which poets used primarily to address their immediate patrons, themselves and other poets. We can get some idea of the situation if we compare the following lines by a successful eighteenth-century poet, Thomas Warton (1728–90), written in 1750, with the prophetic note struck by Blake in the first of his *Songs of Experience* (*c.* 1794). In 'Ode, Sent to a Friend', Warton wrote:

[4]'Preface' to *Lyrical Ballads* (1800), in *Lyrical Ballads*, ed. R.L. Brett and A.R. Jones, London: Methuen (1965), p. 245.

> Ah, mourn, thou loved retreat! No more
> Shall classic steps thy scenes explore!
> When morn's pale rays but faintly peep
> O'er yonder oak-crowned airy steep,
> Who now shall climb its brows to view
> The length of landscape, ever new,
> Where Summer flings, in careless pride,
> Her varied vesture far and wide?
> Who mark, beneath, each village-charm,
> Or grange, or elm-encircled farm;
> The flinty dovecot's crowded roof,
> Watch'd by the kite that sails aloof;
> The tufted pines, whose umbrage tall
> Darkens the long-deserted hall;
> The veteran beech, that on the plain
> Collects at eve the playful train;
> The cot that smokes with early fire,
> The low-roof'd fane's embosom'd spire?

Blake wrote:

> Hear the voice of the bard,
> Who present, past, and future sees –
> Whose ears have heard
> The Holy Word
> That walked among the ancient trees,
>
> Calling the lapsed soul
> And weeping in the evening dew –
> That might control
> The starry pole
> And fallen, fallen light renew.

The most obvious contrast lies in the decorative and obviously dated language of Warton's lines ('morn', 'yonder', 'umbrage', 'fane') where the poet's task appears primarily that of a beautifier, over against the direct and relatively plain language of Blake insisting on the bardic role of the poet, a prophet with authority to pronounce on the major issues of life. One of Warton's chief instruments of beautification is to describe the countryside in recognizably Classical terms; he recasts it to resemble paintings of Italian landscapes then so popular with the English aristocracy and well-to-do middle class. His fashionable lament that 'No more/Shall classic steps thy scenes explore' does not stop him from complying with the tradition. Equally his claim that the landscape is 'ever new' must be set against his intention to describe it in terms instantly recognizable and acceptable to his readership.

It is with these tendencies in particular that we find Wordsworth arguing in the 'Preface' to *Lyrical Ballads*, using by way of illustration Thomas Gray's sonnet, 'In vain to me the smiling mornings shine'. In defiance of the genteel taste and poetic language of the time, Wordsworth suggests that Gray (1716-71) should refer to the sun *as* the sun, and that he gains nothing from dressing it up as 'reddening Phoebus'. Like Blake, Wordsworth recognized that fundamental changes were taking place in society, and consequently his determination to reclaim a central position for the poet led him towards the conviction that poetry was an essentially natural form of expression, rooted in common experience and born of deeply felt emotions. It was the means whereby potentially destructive divisions might be bridged. For Wordsworth it became a matter of bridging, not one of radically reordering society. The poet was the person capable of giving proper expression to such common feelings and sensations. The emphasis on Nature in Wordsworth's poetry arose from his search for the permanent and therefore most trustworthy sources of emotion. The environment of the growing cities did not provide this, the permanent forms of Nature did.

Paradoxically, therefore, while attempting to recapture a public voice for poetry, a voice which expressed a collective consciousness, the Romantic Movement was equally responsible for personalizing poetry in its concern for matters which had as much to do with responses and feelings on the part of individuals, as with awareness operating on a collective, social plain. 'Wordsworth,' writes Abrams, 'may also be accounted the critic whose highly influential writings, by making the feelings of the poet the centre of critical reference, mark a turning-point in English literary theory' (*Abrams* p. 103).

Identifying what seems an inherent contradiction within Romanticism between its public, often moralizing posture, and its tendency towards intense introversion can often carry with it a degree of censure; alternatively it may be argued that its great strength lay precisely in the way that contradictions and tensions were recognized and revealed. Certainly Wordsworth came to believe that for his generation the lessons of the French Revolution lay in unmasking the inadequacy of purely political, material schemes of social regeneration; such ideals – based in man's confidence in the power of his own reason – were doomed to failure unless they operated in conjunction with the deeply considered spiritual, emotional needs of the individuals who went to make up that society. Yet within his work there remains evidence of the suspicion that there might after all be a solution to the problem by way of direct, decisive, essentially political action, rather than through the 'wise passiveness' he strove to cultivate. The poem in which he uses that phrase, 'Expostulation and Reply', along with its companion-piece in *Lyrical Ballads*, 'The Tables Turned', deals with precisely that theme; and repeatedly his awareness of a personal dilemma where wise passivity and political action were concerned surfaces in his creative work, as here in a later, unfinished autobiographical poem, *Home at Grasmere*:

> I cannot at this moment read a tale
> Of two brave Vessels matched in deadly fight
> And fighting to the death, but I am pleased
> More than a wise Man ought to be; I wish,
> I burn, I struggle, and in soul am there.[5]

The suspicion remained that 'wise passiveness' in a poet might effectively become simply passive withdrawal. By the end of the nineteenth century there were those (including Yeats) prepared to argue that, if the Romantic Movement had been a genuinely creative artistic force at its inception, the tendency to opt for withdrawal had brought about its degeneration into a movement characterized by morbid sentimentality, while the ambition of poets like Wordsworth, Coleridge and Shelley to create through their poetry the intellectual climate in which a society in moral and political decline might achieve regeneration had long since been lost in a welter of emotionalism. By 1906, when the *Times Literary Supplement* was reviewing Sturge Moore's *Poems*, the following assessment of Romanticism was relatively commonplace: 'In all the arts romantic ideas and emotions seem to have lost their savour, and now they only satisfy sentimentalists.'[6] Decadence, introversion and insubstantially were among the charges levelled at late Victorian poets like Swinburne, Ernest Dowson, Lional Johnson, Aubrey Beardsley and Oscar Wilde.

Arnold had regretted the 'political, practical character' of Romanticism, implying that great art, while not divorced from its social and political context, operated above the level of day-to-day political considerations. For a cultural model he offered his own idealized vision of the Classical world, and of England in the late sixteenth century. By the turn of the nineteenth century, mid-Victorian poetry (Arnold's included) was being criticized for its habit of tedious moralizing, and also – given by then the emergence of figures like Swinburne, Beardsley and Wilde – for its tendency to encourage the less healthy, escapist aspects of Romanticism. In addition to this there was criticism aimed specifically at late nineteenth-century poetry where Romanticism was understood to have spawned a thoroughly unwholesome school of self-indulgent, morally corrupt writers and artists of the kind W.S. Gilbert ridiculed with such relish in his libretto for the comic opera, *Patience* (1881).

In general terms, therefore, it is possible to see how the critical conditions existed for a comprehensive reaction against Romanticism as represented by the entire period from Wordsworth through to the so-called Decadents of Edwardian England. The Modernist movement, initiated by

---

[5] *Home at Grasmere*, ed. Beth Darlington, Brighton: Harvester (1977) pp. 96–8 11.929–33. MS 'B' 1806.
[6] *TLS* 18 May, 1906. It is worth noting here that the article is quoted in full in *The Literary Notebooks of Thomas Hardy*, two vols., ed. A. Bjork, London: Macmillan (1885) Vol. II pp. 304–6.

the Imagists before the First World War, and dominated by T.S. Eliot after the war, took up this position. Before the war the chief proponents of Imagism were advocating the virtues of brevity and clarity that they associated with Classicism, and Modernism encouraged the critical reappraisal of seventeenth and early eighteenth-century English literature.

The over-all situation was by no means one of a clear break with Romanticism, however. Criticism of late nineteenth-century Romanticism bore a strong resemblance in many ways to the Romantic reaction against late Augustan poetry, not least in its suspicion of sentimentalism. The sense of poetry losing its voice where matters of immediate social and political import were at stake echoed the anxieties of Blake, Wordsworth and Shelley; and Wordsworth's dilemma where the respective virtues of passivity and action were concerned was not to be obliterated by the Modernist wish to turn from a politically informed sense of history towards the goal of an impersonal, intellectualized concept of the universality of art. The post-Modernist period of the 1930s was dominated to a significant degree by W.H. Auden, who, up to the outbreak of the Second World War, published poetry that urged a return to the centre of the political stage for poets committed to the fight against Fascism. In its way, this can be seen as a restatement of the initial Romantic dilemma; Auden, like Wordsworth, was only too well aware that he was in fact writing for a relatively small company of like-minded intellectuals, and like Wordsworth, he was by no means secure in his personal political commitment.

Of the major poets to emerge at the turn of the century, both W.B. Yeats and Thomas Hardy were far from rejecting out of hand the Romantic heritage of English poetry, though both were prepared to be critical of the emanations of Romanticism that had evolved during the nineteenth century.

In his essay *The Symbolism of Poetry* (1900), Yeats (1865–1939) complained that the prevailing critical climate of the times had become dominated by a journalistic frame of mind capable only of contemplating literature in the light of its immediate impact. He saw this superficial critical view being extended to include all great writers of the past. The belief existed, he wrote, that even creative geniuses of the stature of Shakespeare 'talked of wine and women and politics, but never about their art, or never quite seriously about their art.'[7] Yeats's own determination to present art as having always possessed a potentially profound significance for society, and artists as far more 'serious' people than they were given credit for, did not mean that he wished to distance himself completely from the generation of poets who had emerged since Tennyson had ceased to publish in the late 1880s. He owed much to the lyric poetry of the late Victorians, notably that inspired by the Pre-Raphaelite movement, even as Wordsworth had been indebted to many poets of the late Augustan period who brought increasing degrees

---

[7] *The Symbolism of Poetry*, in *W.B. Yeats: Essays and Introductions*, London: Macmillan (1961), pp. 153–64. Hereafter *Symbolism*.

of 'sensibility' to their work. Yeats was also like Wordsworth in that he wished to insist upon the seriousness of the creative process. Our understanding of this may be helped by remembering that where Wordsworth's generation were influenced in this respect by the experience of major political events, Yeats was a committed Irish Nationalist, one who was constantly reviewing the relationship between what he called 'the divine life' and 'the outer life' of the poet; a distinction not without its similarity to Wordsworth's juxtaposition of wise passivity and political commitment (*Symbolism* p. 155).

In the late 1930s, he continued to disparage Victorian poetry, notably that of Tennyson; the Wordsworthian commitment to a social and political role for the poet had degenerated into 'Victorian rhetorical moral fervour' where 'the most famous poetry was often a passage in a poem of some length, perhaps of great length, a poem full of thoughts that might have been expressed in prose.' Tennyson, in common with Swinburne, Arnold and Browning, were at fault in having 'admitted so much psychology, science, moral fervour' into their work.[8]

Just as Wordsworth in the 'Preface' to *Lyrical Ballads* had claimed that emotions summoned up by 'the beautiful and permanent forms of nature' were to liberate poetry from its attachment to the shallow rhetoric of late eighteenth-century picturesque writing, so Yeats came to believe that the rediscovery of Symbolism for poetry would liberate the art from a growing tendency to 'lose itself in externalities of all kinds, in opinion, in declamation, in picturesque writing' (*Symbolism* p. 155). Against the background of the Irish Nationalist movement Yeats fostered a belief in the power of folk-memory, a collective consciousness capable of uniting the otherwise disparate sections of modern society with its complex class structures, and an ever growing urban population which promoted a very different cultural ambiance from that associated with rural community life. As it was impossible to find contemporary themes of a unifying nature in modern society, the poet's task was to invoke through the use of symbols an often submerged awareness of a national identity. Unity is a recurring point of reference for Yeats when he attempts to discuss 'the continuous indefinable symbolism which is the substance of all style':

> ... when sound, and colour, and form are in a musical relation, a beautiful relation to one another, they become as it were one sound, one colour, one form, and evoke an emotion that is made out of their distinct evocations and yet is one emotion. (*Symbolism*, p. 157)

The new poetry, wielding its symbolic power, Yeats believed, would unite 'big house and hovel, college and public house, civil servant – his Gaelic certificate in his pocket – and international bridge-playing women', reminding them all that 'they belong to one nation.'[9] Cairns Craig has

---

[8]*Modern Poetry: A Broadcast*, in Yeats, *Essays and Introductions*, *op. cit.*, pp. 491–508.
[9]Quoted in Cairns Craig, *Yeats, Eliot, Pound and the Politics of Poetry*, London: Croom Helm (1982), p. 276. Hereafter *Craig*.

argued that Yeats's belief in the power of memory to resolve a 'multitudousness ... into unity' is closely linked to the associationist theories of memory that were so influential on poets of the early Romantic period, painfully aware as they were of the divisive forces at work in their own society (*Craig* p. 276). 'This model of the "one in many" and "many in one" ', David Simpson has pointed out, 'is a dominant paradigm in Romantic thought.'[10]

Yeats, profoundly influenced in this early part of his career by the poetry and philosophy of Blake, was attempting to reassert, as his Romantic forbears had done, the essential unity of all things; and just as one major stylistic innovation wrought by the Romantic Movement was the rediscovery of the ballad and short lyric form for serious poetic discourse, so Yeats, in search of a form which would invoke symbolic echoes of a unifying folk-memory, turned from the tedious length of moralizing Victorian verse to ballads of often remarkable lyrical intensity:

> Who dreamed that beauty passes like a dream?
> For these red lips, with all their mournful pride,
> Mournful that no new wonder may betide,
> Troy passed away in one high funeral gleam,
> And Usna's children died.
>
> We and the labouring world are passing by:
> Amid men's souls, that waver and give place
> Like the pale waters in their wintry race,
> Under the passing stars, foam of the sky,
> Lives on this lonely face.
>
> Bow down, archangels, in your dim abode:
> Before you were, or any hearts to beat,
> Weary and kind one lingered by His seat;
> He made the world to be a grassy road
> Before her wandering feet.
> ('The Rose of the World', from *The Rose*, 1893)

The world of history, the 'labouring world', is transient; it is the 'dream'. Beauty, the ultimate truth symbolized by 'the rose of the world', is depicted in a pastoral landscape, passing through the world on 'a grassy road', neither to be created nor destroyed by it.

Blake, reanimating 'Gothic' form to contend against the tyranny of Classical art, was, like Yeats, looking to what he understood as a national heritage of poetry. *Lyrical Ballads*, the volume of poetry by Wordsworth and Coleridge first published in 1798, sought to re-establish a style which

---

[10] David Simpson, *Wordsworth and the Figurings of the Real*, London: Macmillan (1982), p. 122.

both poets then saw as having been debased by writers who used the ballad for shallow, sentimental tales in verse. One of the best known of these poems, Coleridge's *The Rime of the Ancient Mariner*, is at one level an obvious imitation of the manner of a medieval ballad; yet Coleridge uses it to develop ideas that go far beyond what a contemporary reader of medieval pastiche would expect. Wordsworth's 'Simon Lee', on the other hand, seeks to make its point partly through the device of parodying the contemporary eighteenth-century sentimental ballad.

Behind the late eighteenth and early nineteenth-century use of associationism lies an appeal back through memory to a past age in which the nation enjoyed the socially unifying influence of a way of life bound to the land and its seasonal, rural cycle of events. A notion of oneness or wholeness so conceived was understood by Wordsworth to offer a vital controlling influence on man's perception of the social order. It was a means of perception that needed reinstating after the damaging intellectual effects of the French Revolution. His landscapes generally consist of dramatic contrasts which only the poetic sensibility is capable of reconciling, as here with the flatness of the Leven estuary set against the mountains beyond:

> ... Over the smooth sands
> Of Leven's ample aestuary lay
> My journey, and beneath a genial sun,
> With distant prospect among gleams of sky
> And clouds, and intermingled mountain-tops,
> In one inseparable glory clad –
> Creatures of one ethereal substance, met
> In consistory ...

This passage from Book X of *The Prelude* (1805 edition, lines 474–81) occurs in the context of the poet hearing the news of the death of the French Revolutionary leader, Maximillian Robespierre, in 1794. Wordsworth's commitment to the extreme form of political radicalism for which Robespierre stood had at best lasted for only a very short period of his life, and even then has been the subject of some debate.[11] By 1804, when Book X was being written, he had become convinced that Robespierre's philosophy of revolution was grounded in a divisive political creed which failed to recognize the permanently inherent variety, or 'multitudousness', of creation, of which human society was an organic part.

Yeats also believed in the inherent soundness of an agararian society. Like Blake before him, he saw himself as a reincarnation of one of the poets, or 'bards', from the distant Celtic past, 'singing heroic action and "appealing to all natures alike, to the great concourses of the people ..." '

---

[11] See John Williams, *Salisbury Plain: Politics in Wordsworth's Poetry*, in *Literature and History*, Vol. 9:2, Autumn 1983 pp. 164–93.

(*Craig* p. 73). Such a conviction perpetuated the Romantic challenge to an alien Classicism, and was also, in its atavistic nature, rooted in a frame of mind that – while it believed in the need for change – framed its conception of progress in conservative terms. The great cities and the way of life they fostered were never going to disappear, but in order for them and their inhabitants to be assimilated into a unified social organism, it was necessary to evoke the spirit of an ancient wisdom. 'The Man who Dreamed of Faeryland' is modern man who has stumbled upon the ancient world, but tragically cannot comprehend any alternative to his own materialistic society:

> He wandered by the sands of Lissadell;
> His mind ran all on money cares and fears,
> And he had known at last some prudent years
> Before they heaped his grave under the hill;
> But while he passed before a plashy place,
> A lug-worm with its grey and muddy mouth
> Sang that somewhere to the north or west or south
> There dwelt a gay, exulting, gentle race
> Under the golden or the silver skies;
> That if a dancer stayed his hungry foot
> It seemed the sun and moon were in the fruit:
> And at that singing he was no more wise.
> (From The Rose, 1893)

Yeats was of Anglo-Irish stock; through his mother he considered himself a part of the Irish aristocracy, and from her he inherited both his protestantism in religion, and his Republican politics. Much of his childhood was spent in London, where he went to school. In the 1890s he was a member of the Rhymers' Club, and a close friend of Johnson, Dowson and Arthur Symons. Symons, a fellow enthusiast for symbolism (he published *The Symbolist Movement in Literature* in 1899) introduced Yeats to contemporary European literature, to Mallarmé, Calderón and others; but it was as a self-consciously Irish poet committed to traditional forms, implicitly nostalgic, that Yeats's work came to influence the evolution of twentieth-century poetry. He sought to perpetuate that particular strand of the Romantic Movement which had attempted to re-establish poetry as a more universally relevant art to the nation, doing so through the revival of its peculiarly native traditions associated with the metrically regular, rhyming ballad and its variants.

Equally influential in this respect was Thomas Hardy (1840–1928). Hardy's public career as a poet began in 1898 with the publication of *Wessex Poems* when he was fifty-eight. Between then and his death in 1928 he published eight volumes of poetry containing 918 poems. Between 1904 and 1908 he also published *The Dynasts*, 'An Epic Drama of the War with Napoleon' written partly in blank verse, partly in a variety of other metres, and partly in prose. In *Goodbye To All That* (1929) Robert Graves recalled Hardy telling him as a poet that 'All we can do is write on the old themes in the old styles, but try to do it a little better than those who came before us.' The words have become famous, but the implied antagonism towards innovation is misleading. Hardy certainly believed in the short lyric and ballad as the most appropriate form for English poetry, and had little time for modern experimentation with free verse as it was understood to be used by French poets in particular. His recurring use of rural settings also gives the impression of a very traditional attitude. But within that framework Hardy was tirelessly inventive, continually exploring original uses of rhyme and metre, and in reaction to much Victorian poetry attempting, as Michael Schmidt has suggested, to reflect the real world rather than 'offering an alternative world'.[12] Hardy's 'real world' was nevertheless rooted in his awareness of the past; despite that, his sensibility was essentially that of a post-Victorian, 'he was intellectually of this century' (*Schmidt* p. 24), and his attitude was fundamentally pessimistic.

> The moving sun-shapes on the spray,
> The sparkles where the brook was flowing,
> Pink faces, plightings, moonlit May,
> These were the things we wished would stay;
>   But they were going.
>
> Seasons of blankness as of snow,
> The silent bleed of a world decaying,
> The moan of multitudes in woe,
> These were the things we wished would go;
>   But they were staying.
>
> Then we looked closlier at Time,
> And saw his ghostly arms revolving
> To sweep off woeful things with prime,
> Things sinister with things sublime
>   Alike dissolving.[13]

The lyric form, with its metrical regularity and rhyme scheme are indicative of a traditional style; but there is evidence here also of experimentation. The first verse describes the 'poetic' qualities of the rural landscape as objects of misplaced loyalty, 'they were going'. In his description of the things that remain Hardy introduces a phrase that jars poetically because of his unorthodox grammatical use of the word 'bleed', a strategy repeated in the final verse with his idiosyncratic coinage of the word

---

[12] Michael Schmidt, *50 Modern British Poets*, London: Heinemann (1979), p. 24. Hereafter *Schmidt*.
[13] 'Going and Staying', *Late Lyrics* (1922), in *Thomas Hardy: The Complete Poems*, ed. James Gibson, London: Macmillan (1976) pp. 573-4.

'closlier'. In neither verse two nor verse three is the metre allowed the easy flow afforded by the first verse. The final observation that 'Things sinister' and 'sublime' are 'Alike dissolving' is a profoundly unromantic conclusion.

Hardy's originality, often the object of criticism by contemporary reviewers who understood him to be using the 'old styles' ineptly, made him the object of admiration for two otherwise contrasting poetic movements early in the century.

The first self-consciously 'Modernist' poets in England in the twentieth century, calling themselves Imagists, hailed him as a precursor of Modernism, while the Georgian poets – claiming to be equally modern – viewed Hardy's experimentation in a less iconoclastic light than the Imagists, finding in his work a model for their own reinvigorated style of traditional poetry.

Georgian poetry, established through a series of anthologies edited by Edward Marsh after 1911, constituted an attempt to revive the popularity of English poetry at a time when Hardy, Bridges and Masefield were generally respected, but no English poet of any comparable stature was emerging to take their place. The title 'Georgian' arose from the association of Marsh's anthologies with the accession of George V on the death of Edward VII in 1910. The general intention of Marsh was to encourage the writing of poetry very much in the spirit of Hardy's comment to Graves. Among the poets who appeared in the anthologies were Rupert Brooke, Walter de la Mare, W.H. Davies and Edmund Blunden. While Georgian poetry was essentially retrospective, drawing for its images on an imagined English countryside of the past containing the predictable landmarks, 'country cottages, old furniture, moss-covered barns, rose-scented lanes, apple and cherry-orchards',[14] it sought to strike a new and energetic note of patriotism. Before long, the already popular theme of a national heritage threatened by urban growth was to be dramatically intensified by the threat of a European war.

Georgianism was thus a reaction against overly sentimental poetry where it occurred in the mid-Victorian period, and was most certainly set against the aestheticism of the 1890s. At the same time it tended to reinstate a patriotic brand of political conservatism endemic to the work of Wordsworth, Scott, Coleridge and Southey, and to bind this in with its determination – also in common with the early Romantics – of re-establishing a wide readership for poetry. On this last count, sales figures for the Georgian anthologies indicate that it was in no small way successful.

One of the most interesting poets to become associated with the Georgian initiative was Edward Thomas, born in 1878, and killed on active service in 1917. After twenty-two years spent writing books on the countryside, compiling anthologies and writing reviews, he met the American poet, Robert Frost. With Frost's encouragement, he turned to poetry. 'The Owl'

[14]*Georgian Poetry*, ed. James Reeves, Penguin Books (1962), p. xv.

understandably therefore appears both in James Reeves's anthology, *Georgian Poetry* and in Jon Silkin's *First World War Poetry*, reminding us that classification must always be handled with care:

> Downhill I came, hungry, and yet not starved;
> Cold, yet had heat within me that was proof
> Against the North wind; tired, yet so that rest
> Had seemed the sweetest thing under a roof.
>
> Then at the inn I had food, fire, and rest,
> Knowing how hungry, cold, and tired was I.
> All of the night was quite barred out except
> An owl's cry, a most melancholy cry
>
> Shaken out long and clear upon the hill,
> No merry note, nor cause of merriment,
> But one telling me plain what I escaped
> And others could not, that night, as in I went.
>
> And salted was my food, and my repose,
> Salted and sobered, too, by the bird's voice
> Speaking for all who lay under the stars,
> Soldiers and poor, unable to rejoice.[15]

The poem clearly makes use of ideas and images that have a basis in sentimental associations with the countryside, 'Then at the inn I had food, fire, and rest . . .'; but where the first two stanzas reinforce the sense of security such sentiment might encourage, the second two pour 'salt' on the food and the poet's longed-for rest. The final two lines of the poem, however, with their very general reference to 'Soldiers and poor, unable to rejoice', lay Thomas open to the kind of criticism often levelled at Georgian war poets. He does after all enjoy his guilt-complex from a comfortably bucolic vantage point, and the dominant note at the end is one of withdrawal to the shelter of the rural inn, rather than a confrontation with the precise conditions of soldiers and vagrants, and the reasons for those conditions.

What is 'Georgian' in a positive sense about this poem becomes clear if we compare it with two verses from a poem by Sir Henry Newbolt (1862–1938). Newbolt is probably best known as the 'imperialist poet' who wrote 'Drake's Drum' and 'Clifton Chapel', poems expressing an uncritical admiration for what are now generally viewed as the worst aspects of nineteenth-century British imperialism. He lacked Kipling's satirical edge, and has therefore held his place less securely as a poet worthy of serious critical attention, but his verse was very popular throughout the period, and continued to appear in schools' anthologies well on into the 1950s. 'He

---

[15]*First World War Poetry*, ed. Jon Silkin, Penguin Books (1981), p. 93. Hereafter *Silkin*.

Fell Among Thieves' expresses an élitist, sentimentalized picture of life in the English countryside against which 'The Owl' reads as a poem of far greater depth:

> He saw the April noon on his books aglow,
>   The wistaria trailing in at the window wide;
> He heard his father's voice from the terrace below
>   Calling him down to ride.
>
> He saw the gray little church across the park,
>   The mounds that hid the loved and honour'd dead;
> The Norman arch, the chancel softly dark,
>   The brasses black and red.[16]

Rhythmically, Newbolt's poem is far less complex, its relatively clear beat reflects the clarity and simplicity of the idyllic circumstances which surround the memories of childhood. The second verse is the easiest of the two to scan, giving us five heavy stresses in the first three lines (/), and three in the fourth. The short fourth line has the effect of rounding off the verse's statement with a pleasing tidiness:

> He saw. the gray. little church. a-cross. the park,
>   The mounds. that hid. the loved. and hon.our'd dead;
> The Nor.man arch. the chan.cel soft.ly dark,
>   The brass.es black. and red.

The dark is 'soft', and death is a comfortable bed in the churchyard.

'The Owl' scans far less comfortably. The lines conform to a regular pattern of ten syllables, but it is difficult to establish a regular stress pattern. The first line, for example, implies the following rhythm (light stresses are marked ˇ):

> Down-hill I came, hun-gry, and yet not starved;

The first line of the second stanza begins similarly, but then changes:

> Then at the inn I had food, fire, and rest,

Each line of the poem carries five heavy stresses, but they occur at different points, creating in the reader a sense of insecurity which challenges the apparent security implied by the images which predominate in the first two stanzas. The stanza structure which knits the second and fourth lines

---

[16]In *The Oxford Book of Victorian Verse*, ed. Sir Arthur Quiller-Couch, Oxford: The Clarendon Press (1912), pp. 840–1, ll. 17–24.

together with rhyming words imposes an over-all control, but here again, that is compromised by the grammatical run-on from stanza two to three, and by the use of 'And' at the start of stanza four. Although the third stanza finishes with the end of a sentence and a full stop, the effect is to make the first line of stanza four sound as though it is a continuation of the sentence that begins with the third line of stanza two.

Interesting, and indeed 'modern', as all this may perhaps make Thomas's poem seem, to the detractors of Georgian poetry, it was nowhere near enough. The Georgians sustained and developed poetry which retained fundamental links with the Romantic Movement, and its belief in the source of the country's cultural and social stability. The concept of the lyrical ballad which described the English landscape as an embodiment of all that was best in the human spirit informed most of the poetry in the anthologies. Though A.E. Housman was never prepared to contribute to Marsh's anthologies, his sequence of poems published in 1896 as *A Shropshire Lad* epitomized this approach. Despite the widely held contemporary view that the Georgians were indeed the modern poets of their day, Modernism has since come to be defined very differently, and it is with the advent of Modernism that we encounter the attempt to overthrow the influence of Romanticism completely, along with the resurgence of an intense interest in Classicism which had little in common with Arnold's sentimentally idealized vision of Ancient Greece and Rome.

2
Modernism 1900–1930

The most significant attempt to break with established literary traditions before the First World War came from the Imagist school of poets. The Imagist credo, initiated by T.E. Hulme after 1908, developed an explicit rejection not just of late Victorian poetry, but of the fundamental tenets introduced into the theory of poetry by the Romantics. Many definitions of Imagism have been attempted. As its name suggests, the central point of reference is the 'image' itself, clearly stated by the poet to recreate an otherwise inexpressible and unique experience of insight. In that last point lies the crucial differentiation between what Hulme was arguing for, and Yeats's belief in Symbolism. 'No moralizing tone; no reflection on human experience . . .; no striving for the spiritual; no fixed metre or rhyme – but a rhythm organic to the image itself; no narrative – it needs none; no vagueness of abstractions – it would destroy the image.'[1] For Hulme Symbolism was simply a facet of Romanticism, and as such constituted a barrier to genuine poetic discourse. As Raymond Williams has pointed out, Romanticism for Hulme represented a misconceived notion of society and social evolution based in the humanist tradition that saw the perfectibility of the State growing out of the gradual perfectibility of individuals. Hulme's attack on the Romantic Movement amounted to an attack on the whole matrix of political, philosophical and literary ideas that had come to dominate European thought since the Renaissance.[2]

Latter-day Romantics had indulged increasingly in sentimentalism as a consequence of the belief that 'the individual is an infinite reservoir.' The individual, Hulme countered, 'is an extraordinarily fixed and limited animal whose nature is absolutely constant' (*Jones* p. 29). This reaction to Romanticism has as its alternative model Classical art, and Hulme prophesied that '. . . a period of dry, hard, classical verse is coming' (*Jones* p. 29). 'It's straight talk,' Ezra Pound wrote of Hilda Doolittle's Imagist poetry, 'straight as the Greek!' (*Jones* p. 17).

After a century of uncertainty and debate, the Imagists launched an unequivocal attack on every aspect of Romanticism. They were an Anglo-

---

[1] T.E. Hulme (1883–1917), quoted in *Imagist Poetry*, ed. Peter Jones, Penguin Books (1972), p. 31. Hereafter *Jones*.
[2] Raymond Williams, *Culture and Society 1780–1950*, Penguin Books (1963), pp. 191–5.

American group, Ezra Pound (1885-1972) being the most successfully vociferous of the Americans, and as such they challenged the concept of a specifically English or British school of poetry. They encouraged the use of experimental poetic forms, favouring above all the *vers libre* (free verse) technique. The Imagists were particularly impressed by the French *vers libre* poets of the latter part of the nineteenth century (including Jules Laforgue and Émile Verhaeren), though in America Walt Whitman had begun to publish free verse in the mid nineteenth century. In England, despite his distrust of modernity, Arnold's skilful use of the Classical Pindaric Ode form could often create the effect of free verse, where all preordained controls in relation to metre, line length and rhyme are abandoned. Imagism emphasized the uniqueness of each poem, a view that differed radically from Yeats's understanding of symbolic significance, and it denied the poet a philosophizing, moralizing role, what Pound referred to dismissively as 'slither' (*Jones* p. 17). Pound was among those Imagists who recognized in Hardy's use of overtly traditional form a note of dissent which directed it away from the sentimental optimism and nostalgia of Romantics and Symbolists, giving the poems a modernistic clarity of vision, often as not achieved by the startling juxtaposition of images. He confidently differentiated Hardy's work from his contemporaries, who still produced 'a doughy mess of third-hand Keats, Wordsworth, heaven knows what, fourth-hand Elizabethan sonority blunted, half-melted, lumpy' (*Jones* p. 14).

It is tempting to see something more than chance giving rise to Pound's omission of any specific examples of poets between the Elizabethans and Wordsworth. Whether or not he consciously side-stepped the Augustan Classical period, this is a reminder that the Imagists were not enemies of tradition. Hulme and Pound were opposed to what the Romantics had made of tradition, and offered as alternatives Grecian Classicism and the art forms of eastern cultures, notably early Japanese poetry, of which the brief 'haiku' formed a model for many Imagist poems.

Despite Pound's scorn for Symbolism, he at least shared a fundamentally conservative ideology with Yeats which originated in their common regard for the significance of the past, as perpetuated through a process of memory. But Pound went on to attack emotionalism, and to reject any concern for a particularly public voice. Imagism highlights what was evidently then a widespread belief, felt in a variety of ways, that for poetry to function as it should, it must be freed from an unhealthily strong commitment to the feelings and the passions of its time.

Hilda Doolittle's poem 'Oread' is representative of the Imagist aesthetic at its most severe. H.D. (1886-1961), as she became known, not infrequently wrote at greater length, but in this poem she was able to use extraordinary economy to capture the image. The unlikely juxtaposition of sea and pines is designed to liberate the mind from its preconceptions in order that it might experience the uniqueness of the moment. To suggest a 'design' upon the reader though, is to question the poem's integrity, for reflection was not a part of Imagist practise:

> Whirl up, sea –
> Whirl your pointed pines,
> Splash your great pines
> On our rocks,
> Hurl your green over us,
> Cover us with your pools of fir.
> (*Jones* p. 62)

The form of the poem is analysable only in so far as it relates to the image, thus *vers libre* is appropriate, where a preordained metrical and rhyming structure is not. To understand how rhythm operates in 'Oread', it will help to look at the way Herbert Read, a poet and critic influenced by Imagist theory, attempted to define poetry. 'The poem,' he wrote, 'is a rhythmical figure, complete in itself . . .':

> A poem is therefore to be defined as a structure of words whose sound constitutes a rhythmical unity, complete in itself, irrefragible, unanalysable, completing its symbolic references within the ambit of its sound-effect.[3]

There can be no doubt that Pound would have loved to have had the opportunity to 'modernize' Hardy, as in due course he did Yeats, and to some extent T.S. Eliot. But Hardy was no recruit to Modernism; his concern to invoke essentially timeless forces operating on human destiny within the context of familiar settings (often, but by no means exclusively rural), and to do so using poetic forms which at least appear to be easily recognizable, often creates a tension within his work which exemplifies the continuing debate between poets who recognize the merits of a Romantic heritage, and those who yearn for the virtues associated with Classicism.

The Imagists' determination to stand clear of any stylistic association with the Romantic tradition tended towards a poetic that was endemically 'difficult', and in encouraging the idea of a poem as something detached from the immediate circumstances of its production, they encouraged also the idea of the poet as a writer emotionally detached from his or her work. Poetry which is now seen as belonging to the Modernist movement of 1900–1930 was written for the most part in the shadow of a literary crisis identified to a large extent through the debate insisted on by Imagists over the relationship between poet and poem, and then between poet, poem and reader. It was the next stage of the nineteenth-century debate over the merits of the Romantic Movement initiated by Matthew Arnold. The literary crisis was one which – not surprisingly given the circumstances in

---

[3]Herbert Read (1893–1968), *Collected Poems*, London: Faber & Faber (1966), p. 273.

which the Romantic Movement had first developed – owed much to the social and political circumstances of the early 1900s.

England was taking on the appearance of a nation increasingly threatened by deep social divisions that the liberal humanism of the late nineteenth century was unable to bridge. Liberal humanism has become a convenient formula for describing the ideal of society fostered by Romanticism throughout the nineteenth century; it was based upon 'an assumed harmony among men's varying rational desires, which, when not interfered with, reflect the pre-established harmonies to be found in nature.'[4] Such a view rested in the compliant recognition of a society with clearly defined class distinctions, where the more privileged were trusted to perform their duties in a spirit of paternalism. The concept of Empire, given its classic apologia by Sir John Seeley in *The Expansion of England in the Eighteenth Century* (1883), embodied a concrete expression of this ideal.

The literature of the nineteenth century revealed as much doubt as it did optimism about the effectiveness of the liberal humanist position, with Darwin, Marx and Freud among the major influences on philosophies which in different ways contributed to the growing sense of crisis late in the century. Within the arena of imperial relations, the crisis was initially registered through the Boer War of 1899–1902, and then by the deterioration of Britain's position in India. At home, the industrial revolution had initiated a process of profound change within the class structure of the country that had gone on throughout the century. The eighteenth century had seen the rise to power of a number of middle-class families through successful careers in trade and banking which accelerated the shift of political power and influence away from its traditional aristocratic base rooted in an agrarian economy. In the nineteenth century, there evolved the important additional factor of a self-conscious, increasingly unionized working class, a group potentially antagonistic to the traditional ordering of English political life in a way the rising middle class of the eighteenth century were not.

Victorian novelists depicted the new middle-class industrialists with mixed feelings, and the workers they employed with often undisguised anxiety. One of the best known accounts of the threat to society which the working class could become occurs in Charles Dickens's *Hard Times* (1854). In *Bleak House* (1852–3) the focus of Dickens's satire had been the aristocracy, or that section of it personified by Sir Leicester Dedlock, who is incapable of comprehending how times have changed. The ageing, effete baronet is confronted by one of the new industrialists, Mr Rouncewell the ironmaster. Though Rouncewell is a type not yet fully understood or trusted by Dickens, he nevertheless represents the shrewd, positive man of the modern world on whom responsibility for order and progress must

---

[4] G.H. Bantock, in *The Pelican Guide to English Literature*, vol. VII, *The Modern Age*, ed. Boris Ford, Penguin Books (1964), p. 23. Hereafter *Pelican Guide VII*.

ultimately depend. When he criticizes the local school at Chesney Wold, where Sir Leicester's crumbling home and estate is situated, he prompts a series of alarming reflections in 'the Dedlock mind':

> From the village school of Chesney Wold, intact as it is this minute, to the whole framework of society: from the whole framework of society, to the aforesaid framework receiving tremendous cracks in consequence of people (ironmasters, lead-mistresses, and what not) not minding their catechism, and getting out of the station unto which they are called, necessarily and for ever, according to Sir Leicester's rapid logic, the first station in which they happen to find themselves; and from that, to their educating other people out of *their* stations, and so obliterating the landmarks, and opening the floodgates, and all the rest of it; this is the swift progress of the Dedlock mind.
>
> (Chapter 28)

For all the apparent immobility which characterizes Sir Leicester's antiquated and anomalous concept of social degree, what alarmed contemporary observers of the newly emerging class divisions was the quality of unprecedented rigidity they exhibited, the consequence of which was to threaten the total alienation of a significant proportion of the population. This meant that from the first, the optimism born of Britain's role as the first industrial nation could equally be matched by a strongly felt mood of pessimism where the future was concerned.

The problems which faced British society by the turn of the century were variously registered through the literature: by John Galsworthy's *The Man of Property* (1906), and in his play *Strife* (1909); by H.G. Wells in *The History of Mr Polly* (1910); by Conrad who wrote of the dark political world of anarchistic terrorism in *The Secret Agent* (1907); by Arthur Morrison in three novels, of which *The Children of the Jago* (1896) is the best known; and by E.M. Forster, whose *Howard's End* (1910) contains the desperate plea for us 'only [to] connect'. Forster's work is often cited as the clearest statement of the liberal humanist beset with doubts: the world, he wrote, 'is a globe of men who are trying to reach one another . . . by the help of goodwill plus culture and intelligence' (*Pelican Guide VII* p. 27).

The debate on Romanticism which had been going on throughout the period, must be set within the context of this social and political debate. The response of which Modernism is the literary symptom in the early twentieth century – for all its antagonism to the Romantic Movement – may be seen as in some ways analogous to the response of the Romantics to the political and social crises of their own time. In both cases it was a response that embodied a significant degree of caution, if not political conservatism. It is well worth recalling what effect the radical political ideas engendered by the American and French Revolutions had had on the first Romantics by way of comparison with the views of Modernists like Pound and Eliot.

Poets as apparently diverse in belief and temperament as Wordsworth and Shelley believed that the majority of people within their society were as yet insufficiently educated to be able to cope with the practical application of the radical libertarian ideals at the heart of the revolutionary process. Wordsworth saw a necessary – if intermediary – role for the enlightened 'few/For patrimonial honour set apart' (*Prelude* Book IX, 1805, l. 335); while in his Preface to *Prometheus Unbound* (1819) Shelley wrote:

> My purpose has hitherto been simply to familiarize the highly refined imagination of the more select classes of poetical readers with beautiful idealisms of moral excellence; aware that until the mind can love, and admire, and trust, and hope, and endure, reasoned principles of moral conduct are seeds cast upon the highway of life which the unconscious passenger tramples into the dust, although they would bear the harvest of his happiness.

Modernism likewise contained within its appeal to tradition and its reappraisal of the poet's true function and identity, a concern to establish an authoritative voice capable of fulfilling an affirmative, socially unifying role. The extent to which a crucial change had taken place since the early 1800s in the conception of this authoritative role is particularly evident in the case of Pound. Social unity was no longer to be realistically conceived of as ultimately the property of the common consciousness. It was to be supplied – and indefinitely maintained – by strong leadership from above. The appeal of Fascism for both Yeats and Pound was considerable, and after the war Pound's support for Mussolini's régime in Italy became something of a literary scandal. Yeats's nationalism, for all its nostalgic yearnings for an organic community life located in the rural past, bore the stamp of his aristocratic heritage, and remained essentially élitist. After the war he moved progressively further away from the Romantic optimism of his earlier period. On the eve of the war he had met Pound, and was prepared to listen to the younger poet's views on modern poetry as his own faith in political regeneration wavered. The failure of the Easter Rising in Ireland of 1916 was perhaps the most important political event to influence the redirection of Yeats's work away from poetry written to sustain his Romantic vision of a unified society.

Michael Schmidt's account of Yeats after his time spent with Pound is revealing, emphasizing as it does Yeats's authoritative stance and his suspicion of moralizing, a concern which highlights the crisis of confidence in the Romantic tradition and its political implications. It is revealing also in that Schmidt, an Editorial Director of Carcanet Press, has himself expressed an approval for contemporary poetry which contends for authoritarian ideals:[5]

---

[5]See David Trotter, *The Making of the Reader*, London: Macmillan (1984), pp. 237–8. Hereafter *Trotter*.

Responsibilities (1914) was published two years after Yeats and Pound became friends. Pound's influence may be felt in the Chinese dedicatory couplet, but more in the new tautness, the new way ideas are realized not by moralizing symbols but in the symbols themselves. There is a new authority in the public tone he adopts in some of the poems. He experiments with the severe satire of the bardic poets when he assaults bourgeois philistinism and chastises the misled working classes. He contrasts the art patrons of the Renaissance and the Renaissance audience with the boorish, penny-pinching public servants, the unresponsive public. . . . The new vigour of the verse is reflected in the precision and concreteness of the imagery, the apparently more real passions the poems express, and in the active verb forms. (*Schmidt* p. 53)

Pound's greatest 'discovery' was made in 1914, when he encountered the work of a poet who was subsequently to become the major voice of the Modernist movement, T.S. Eliot. Eliot's work brought together many of the most important strands of critical discontent with Romanticism.

Born in St Louis, Missouri in 1888, Eliot began to write while he was a student at Harvard. In 1908 he read Symons's *The Symbolist Movement in Literature*, and through Symons he discovered the French poet, Jules Laforgue. Laforgue was more than an enthusiasm for Eliot; writing in *The Criterion* over twenty years later, he claimed that *The Symbolist Movement* and his own subsequent study of Laforgue had influenced the course of his life. Quite apart from being able to identify closely with Laforgue himself, 'reticent, scrupulous, correct both in dress and manner', he was drawn to the poetry for its 'denial of conventional feeling . . . both in its ironic scepticism about romantic passion,' and in the way it reflected the poet's 'refusal to reveal or even to take seriously his own.'[6] In 1910 Eliot was writing *The Love Song of J. Alfred Prufrock* and the *Preludes*. He was also becoming increasingly fascinated by Buddhism, which enabled him to reflect further on a philosophy of freedom from passion and desire, the quest for *Nirvana*. In 1914 a Sheldon Travelling Fellowship gave him the chance to return to Europe after an earlier visit in 1910. Following a rapid tour through Belgium, Italy and Germany, he arrived in London in August, and in September – at the suggestion of a friend, Conrad Aiken – he visited Ezra Pound.

From the manuscripts Pound then read, he recognized a kindred Imagist spirit who had begun quite independently to develop a distinctly modern style, one which had not gone down at all well with the English poets Eliot had met, notably Harold Monro, who had described *Prufrock* as 'absolutely insane' (*Ackroyd* p. 55). Pound's influence lay principally in encouraging Eliot to strip away all but the barest essentials in his work, 'modernizing' his style still further in the way he had encouraged Yeats to remould his

[6]Peter Ackroyd, *T.S. Eliot*, London: Hamish Hamilton (1984), p. 34. Hereafter *Ackroyd*.

symbolism. There is a more than coincidental resemblance between the style of Yeats's 'Easter 1916' and that of Eliot in, for example, *Prufrock* (eventually published in 1917). 'Easter 1916' begins with the following lines:

> I have met them at close of day
> Coming with vivid faces
> From counter or desk among grey
> Eighteenth-century houses.
> I have passed with a nod of the head
> Or polite meaningless words,
> Or have lingered awhile and said
> Polite meaningless words,
> And thought before I had done
> Of a mocking tale or gibe
> To please a companion
> Around the fire at the club . . .
> (From *Michael Robartes and the Dancer*, 1921)

Eliot's *Prufrock* begins:

> Let us go then, you and I,
> When the evening is spread out against the sky
> Like a patient etherized upon a table;
> Let us go, through certain half-deserted streets,
> The muttering retreats
> Of restless nights in one-night cheap hotels
> And sawdust restaurants with oyster-shells:
> Streets that follow like a tedious argument
> Of insidious intent
> To lead you to an overwhelming question . . .
> Oh, do not ask, 'What is it?'
> Let us go an make our visit.
> (From *Prufrock and Other Observations*, 1917)

Despite the use both poets make of rhyme, and of a strong rhythmical quality moving through the lines, the 'polite meaningless words' and the 'tedious argument/Of insidious intent' depict a common vision of a fragmented society where the Romantic ideal of perceiving homogeneity is profoundly unrealistic and inappropriate. What gives these two extracts their similar sound is primarily the similarity of attitude struck by both poets from the first lines; the authoritative 'I' heralds a post-Romantic, cynical observer standing to one side (or even slightly above) the commonalty. The task of the Modernist was to reflect the discontinuities of the modern world, and like Arnold, Eliot came to believe that the intellectual atmosphere in which Romanticism had developed had been a seriously damaging one for the artist. He joined with those who criticized Tennyson, describing him as 'a very fair example of a poet almost wholly encrusted with opinion'; Blake, on the other hand, he chose to believe 'approached everything with a mind unclouded by current opinions.' The artist's education, he wrote, 'is one that is hindered rather than helped by the ordinary processes of society which constitute education for the ordinary man.'

Blake interested Eliot to the extent that his poetry appeared to confirm the fact that no matter how gifted the individual poet, great art could only be produced and sustained where the cultural climate was favourable. The eighteenth century provided evidence of a decline in a healthy climate for artists, and Romanticism marked its demise; Blake in the last analysis was a victim: 'What his genius required, and what it sadly lacked, was a framework of accepted and traditional ideas.'[7] Such a framework freed artists from an unhealthy reliance on their personal emotions and opinions. In a passage from his essay *Tradition and the Individual Talent* (1919) where Eliot clearly has Wordsworth in mind, he sums up his attack on Romanticism by insisting that 'Poetry is not a turning loose of emotion, but an escape from emotion; it is not the expression of personality, but an escape from personality' (*Eliot S.E.* p. 21).

Stylistically this implied a rejection of the nineteenth-century concept of what constituted 'traditional' English poetic forms and subjects, particularly as they had been affirmed in the Georgian evocation of a social fabric underpinned by reassuringly secure images of rural life. The twentieth century had only fragments to offer, 'odds and ends' as Eliot described it in his essay on Blake, for the expression of which coherent, regularly rhymed verses with an ordered metre were inappropriate. *Vers Libre*, avoiding if possible the tendency of the English language to settle into metrical regularity, met the Modernist poet's need. Coherence existed, but it was not to be found in the context of modern society. Eliot did not reject symbolism as Yeats had done, but he did not see in it – as Yeats had – a means of realizing a unity otherwise hidden, or masked by contemporary developments. His poetry and criticism reveal a search for evidence of art produced within 'a framework of accepted and traditional ideas', and it was therefore not surprising that he came to define his own position as allied to three specific 'traditions': 'classicist, royalist and anglo-catholic' (*Ackroyd*, p. 41).

His lasting enthusiasm for Dante arose from precisely this search:

> Dante's universality is not solely a personal matter. The Italian language, and especially the Italian language in Dante's age, gains much by being the product of universal Latin. . . . When you read modern

---

[7] Quotations from *William Blake* (1920), in T.S. Eliot, *Selected Essays*, London: Faber & Faber (1951), pp. 317–22. Hereafter *Eliot S.E.*

philosophy, in English, French, German and Italian, you must be struck by national or racial differences of thought: modern languages *tend* to separate abstract thought (mathematics is now the only universal language); but medieval Latin tended to concentrate on what men of various races and lands could think together.

(*Dante*, in *Eliot S.E.* p. 239)

Dante's *Divine Comedy* (completed just before the poet's death in 1321) became a recurring point of reference in Eliot's poetry. Its influence is probably best known for the use he made of the *Inferno* sections when describing post-war London in *The Waste Land*:

> Unreal City,
> Under the brown fog of a winter dawn,
> A crowd flowed over London Bridge, so many,
> I had not thought death had undone so many.
> Sighs, short and infrequent, were exhaled,
> And each man fixed his eyes before his feet.
> (*The Waste Land*: I. 'The Buriel of the Dead' ll. 60–5)

Like both Yeats and Pound, Eliot found himself drawn to reflect on the merits of Fascism in the 1920s, though anything like serious political commitment hardly seems evident from the statement he published in the *Criterion* of 1929:

> I confess to a preference for fascism in practice, which I dare say most of my readers share; and I will not admit this preference is itself wholly irrational. I believe that the fascist form of unreason is less remote from my own than is that of the communists, but that my own is a more reasonable form of unreason.

(Quoted in *Craig* p. 8)

Eliot was responding (at a somewhat higher degree of sophistication than Sir Leicester Dedlock) to the protracted breakdown of the social structures of pre-industrial society, where the class distinctions of a hierarchical society grounded in inherited wealth, 'an organic aristocracy based on land and a culture without ethnic differentiation' (*Craig* p. 9), provided the basis for an art which rose above personal, opinionated statement to become part of that process described in the essay on Dante as 'thinking together'. After the English Civil War of the seventeenth century (an aptly critical moment in history for a monarchist and anglo-catholic), there developed what Eliot called a 'dissociation of sensibility' (*The Metaphysical Poets*, *Eliot S.E.* p. 288). Imagists and Georgians alike perceived this 'dissociation of sensibility' within society, understanding it to mean the loss of a sense of community as organic, over and above its necessary social divisions, where certain sections of the community were materially and politically priviledged at the expense of others. Once this sense of a fundamentally common existence for all was lost, art would inevitably begin to suffer from divided purposes and modes of discourse. The two groups reacted very differently; Georgians like Brooke, Masefield, de la Mare, Thomas and Blunden in their various ways sustained nostalgic links with the Romantic tradition; Modernists like Eliot looked further back in time for the roots of literary tradition and stressed the point that art was the product of a universal human endeavour rather than of nostalgic musings among English country lanes and fields. What both groups had in common, however, was a tendency to become politically reactionary in their views.

This reaction on the part of a highly talented minority among poets in England against Romanticism and the liberal humanist view of social evolution did not herald a Modernist victory in aesthetics. The course of events was undoubtedly influenced by the First World War, which was responsible for creating a situation where the persisting class distinctions within British society were subjected to a uniquely close scrutiny. Distrust and suspicion of those traditionally in positions of power was confirmed by the wartime image of the bungling statesman and the incompetent or callous General who kept well clear of the trenches. At the front it became possible for those of both high and low estate to experience a situation where peacetime class consciousness was replaced by the practical distinction between those who fought and those who stayed at home. This temporary realignment of allegiance was widely enough experienced to ensure that it would never be possible to return to anything like the situation as it was before the war, though it was by no means radical enough to initiate revolutionary changes in the social structure. Richard Aldington, a member of the Imagist group, drew attention to the levelling consequences of the experience of active service in his poem, 'Trench Idyll'.

Aldington's free verse avoids any tendency towards a settled rhythm, and thus emphasizes the bleakness of the situation, idyllic only in so far as the poem describes a momentary lull in the fighting when two soldiers have the opportunity to compare their experiences:

> We sat together in the trench,
> He on a lump of frozen earth
> Blown in the night before,
> I on an unexploded shell;
> And smoked and talked, like exiles . . .

If there is a distinction to be drawn between the two men, it is not to be done in terms of rank or class, only in terms of the horror each has experienced. In the light of this, the knowledge we gain of their relative ranks – withheld until the final line of the poem – comes as a calculatedly surprising revelation for two men who have discoursed as social equals:

> 'It's rather cold here, sir, suppose we move?'
> (*Silkin* p. 143)

After the war, with Eliot as yet hardly known, Ezra Pound a figure associated with the avant-garde, and Yeats and Hardy by no means writing, or being read, as 'Modernists', the 'new' poetry was still essentially Georgian. Anthologies from this group continued to appear until 1922, and tradition rather than innovation dominated the London literary scene; nostalgia laced with symbolism rather than cold, hard classicism. Modernism influenced post-war poetry by a slow process of osmosis. The war had brought Imagist and Georgian sensibilities into a common crucible; a longing for peace, and memories of a lost English way of life tended to erode the Imagist ideal of clarity; anger and disillusionment with existing social structures turned Georgian nostalgia into something more akin to the irony of Modernism. Siegfried Sassoon (1886–1967), schooled in the Georgian tradition before the war, exploded the myths of jingoistic patriotism without departing significantly from traditional forms. Jon Silkin's assessment of Sassoon is to see him as nevertheless potentially a more modern poet than the stylistically innovative Wilfred Owen. Owen (1893–1918) had been influenced by French poetry before the war, and proved himself a master of para and consonant rhyme. Silkin's contention is, however, that the dominant note in his poetry remains one of nostalgic regret, and that he never achieved the more precise social focus of Sassoon (*Silkin* pp. 31–2).

In Wilfred Owen's 'The Show' (*Silkin* pp. 188–9) we can appreciate his tendency to what Silkin calls an 'Olympian compassion':

> My soul looked down from a vague height, with Death,
> As unremembering how I rose or why,
> And saw a sad land, weak with sweats of dearth,
> Gray, cratered like the moon with hollow woe,
> And pitted with great pocks and scabs of plagues.
>
> Across its beard, that horror of harsh wire,
> There moved thin caterpillars, slowly uncoiled.
> It seemed they pushed themselves to be as plugs
> Of ditches, where they writhed and shrivelled, killed.
>
> By them had slimy paths been trailed and scraped
> Round myriad warts that might be little hills.
>
> From gloom's last dregs these long-strung creatures
>   crept,
> And vanished out of dawn down hidden holes.
>
> (And smell came up from those foul openings
> As out of mouths, or deep wounds deepening.)

On dithering feet up-gathered, more and more,
Brown strings, towards strings of gray, with bristling
  spines,
All migrants from green fields, intent on mire.

Those that were gray, of more abundant spawns,
Ramped on the rest and ate them and were eaten.

I saw their bitten backs curve, loop, and straighten.
I watched those agonies curl, lift, and flatten.

Whereat, in terror what that sight might mean,
I reeled and shivered earthward like a feather.

And Death fell with me, like a deepening moan.

And He, picking a manner of worm, which half had hid
Its bruises in the earth, but crawled no further,
Showed me its feet, the feet of many men,
And the fresh-severed head of it, my head.

The para-rhymes (as in 'Death . . . dearth', and 'uncoiled . . . killed') along with the basically iambic ($\smile\,/$) ten syllable line, provide a suitably definite yet illusive, ghostly form of control for the poem. But it is, literally, an over-view. The ghastliness of the detail is held at a distance, the surreal image of the landscape as a decomposing face attacked by caterpillars shocks, but also by virtue of its artistic ingenuity, initiates a response where the 'poetry' and the meaning are inclined to stand in a competing relationship for our attention. In the final four lines, the close view of the horror effectively personalizes the statement; a terrible fate for the poet himself, while the fate of the many remains indistinct, as it was inclined to in Thomas's 'The Owl'.

This is not to argue with the genuineness of Owen's response, nor to suggest that he was not the purveyor of powerful, disturbing poetry. Compared with Aldington's 'Trench Idyll', however, the Georgian respect for a traditional poetic of phrase and rhythm is very marked. The nostalgic touch of 'All migrants from green fields', for example, is typically Georgian, as is the mannered simile of Death falling 'like a deepening moan'.

In other poems, Owen consciously adopted what he recognized as 'Sassoon's style', distinct from his own in its direct recourse to bitter anger, and the use of simpler language and ballad metre:

> He dropped, more sullenly, than wearily,
>   Became a lump of stench, a clot of meat,
>   And none of us could kick him to his feet.
> He blinked at my revolver, blearily.

> He didn't seem to know a war was on,
>   Or see or smell the bloody trench at all . . .
>   Perhaps he saw the crowd at Caxton Hall,
> And that is why the fellow's pluck's all gone –
>
> Not that the Kaiser frowns imperially.
>   He sees his wife, how cosily she chats;
>   Not his blue pal there, feeding fifty rats.
> Hotels he sees, improved materially;
>
> Where ministers smile ministerially.
>   Sees Punch still grinning at the Belcher bloke;
>   Bairnsfather, enlarging on his little joke,
> While Belloc prophecies of last year, serially.
>
> We sent him down at last, he seemed so bad,
>   Although a strongish chap and quite unhurt.
>   Next day I heard the Doc's fat laugh: 'That dirt
> You sent me down last night's just died. So glad!'
>   ('The Dead-Beat', *Silkin* pp. 181–2)

The poem insists on the immediacy of its anger, introducing specific references in verse four to those fighting the war from armchairs at home: the bland patriotism of *Punch Magazine*, the non-combatant poet, Hilaire Belloc. But it has an uneasy air of contrivance to it, especially in the awkward last two lines of the final verse where the unnatural coinage of 'fat laugh', for all the irony of its combined figurative and literal meanings, is out of place in a poem which aims at reproducing colloquial discourse. The tongue-twisting 'last night's just died', and the abruptness of 'So glad!' are equally unconvincing, although the intention to underline a mood of cruel indifference is clear.

Where Owen used ballad form most successfully, it was without the element of parody:

> There was a whispering in my hearth,
>   A sigh of the coal,
> Grown wistful of a former earth
>   It might recall.

This is the opening of a remarkable poem, 'Miners' (*Silkin* pp. 185–6), the meaning of which turns on the gradual movement from the subject of mining coal – a mysterious process suggesting present-day man's connection with the distant past – to the fate of soldiers in the 'dark pits/Of war':

> I thought of some who worked dark pits
>   Of war, and died
> Digging the rock where Death reputes
>   Peace lies indeed.
>
> Comforted years will sit soft-chaired
>   In rooms of amber;
> The years will stretch their hands, well-cheered
>   By our lives' ember.
>
> The centuries will burn rich loads
>   With which we groaned,
> Whose warmth shall lull their dreaming lids,
>   While songs are crooned.
> But they will not dream of us poor lads,
>   Lost in the ground.

Beneath the serenity of 'Comforted years' lies the profoundly disturbing vision of a warming peacetime fire made not from coal, but from the lives of soldiers. Just as the dangers and social injustices associated with the extraction of coal are rarely considered once the fire is lit, so will the sacrifice of young men at the front be swiftly forgotten in the future.

The influence of Sassoon is discernable elsewhere, compromising Owen's more highly wrought use of language with an attention to detail that enhances his naturally reflective style. In 'Mental Cases', for example, he describes men driven insane by their experiences in the trenches, combining the solemnity of blank verse form with a scarcely suppressed degree of Sassoon-like anger:

> Therefore still their eyeballs shrink tormented
> Back into their brains, because on their sense
> Sunlight seems a bloodsmear; night comes blood-black;
> Dawn breaks open like a wound that bleeds afresh.
> – Thus their heads wear this hilarious, hideous,
> Awful falseness of set-smiling corpses.
>   (*Silkin* p. 195)

While Owen forged a significantly distinctive style, considerably influenced by the French poetry he read, Sassoon was never to become a stylistic innovator. In everything but his determination to portray the horrific reality of life in the trenches, he remained a poet in the Georgian mould. His convictions, coupled with his mastery of poetic forms, were more than sufficient to produce poetry of an original kind for the period. The traditional poetic forms of the pre-war years could be – and were – subverted as an effective means of satirizing the attitudes they enshrined. In 'Suicide in the Trenches', for example, we can appreciate the Sassoon that Owen was attempting to emulate in 'The Dead-Beat':

> I knew a simple soldier boy
> Who grinned at life in empty joy,
> Slept soundly through the lonesome dark,
> And whistled early with the lark.
>
> In winter trenches, cowed and glum,
> With crumps and lice and lack of rum,
> He put a bullet through his brain.
> No one spoke of him again.
>
> You smug-faced crowds with kindling eye
> Who cheer when soldier lads march by,
> Sneak home and pray you'll never know
> The hell where youth and laughter go.[8]

If Sassoon appears to be the enemy of many Georgian assumptions, his poetry can nevertheless reveal him as equally the prisoner of much that Georgianism ideologically stood for. A comparison between two poems illustrates this well.

In 'Break of Day' (*Sassoon* p. 102–3), Sassoon describes a soldier during his last few moments waiting for the commencement of a dawn offensive. As he waits, he dreams of times past in England when he has waited for a fox to break cover and the hunt to start. His description of the trenches is uncompromising, 'Where men are crushed like clods, and crawl to find/ Some crater for their wretchedness'; but the major part of the poem is taken up with an idyllic description of the hunt:

> He sniffs the chilly air; (his dreaming starts),
> He's riding in a dusty Sussex lane
> In quiet September; slowly night departs;
> And he's a living soul, absolved from pain.
> Beyond the brambled fences where he goes
> Are glimmering fields with harvest piled in sheaves,
> And tree-tops dark against the stars grown pale;
> Then, clear and shrill, a distant farm-cock crows;
> And there's a wall of mist along the vale
> Where willows shake their watery-sounding leaves,
> He gazes on it all, and scarce believes
> That earth is telling its old peaceful tale . . .

War is far from being the glorious call to duty that it had seemed to Rupert Brooke on the eve of the conflict; but our revulsion is achieved by summoning up an idealized picture of the life lived by the English gentry

---

[8] Siegfried Sassoon, *The War Poems*, Arranged and Introduced by Rupert Hart-Davis, London: Faber & Faber (1983), p. 119. Hereafter *Sassoon*.

every bit as anachronistic as anything produced by the Georgians, and with the same inescapable note of privilege that informed Newbolt's 'He Fell Among Thieves'. The easy flow of the iambic pentameter carries with it no special sense of irony, it serves here to confirm the country-life idyll that makes war such an obscenity. Each stanza uses the arbitrary rhyme scheme of the Pindaric Ode, a form favoured in the nineteenth century by Matthew Arnold.

A poem which describes a similar situation, but in a very different way, is Isaac Rosenberg's 'Break of Day in the Trenches' (*Silkin* p. 208–9):

> The darkness crumbles away –
> It is the same old druid Time as ever.
> Only a live thing leaps my hand –
> A queer sardonic rat –
> As I pull the parapet's poppy
> To stick behind my ear.
> Droll rat, they would shoot you if they knew
> Your cosmopolitan sympathies.
> Now you have touched this English hand
> You will do the same to a German –
> Soon, no doubt, if it be your pleasure
> To cross the sleeping green between.
> It seems you inwardly grin as you pass
> Strong eyes, fine limbs, haughty athletes
> Less chanced than you for life,
> Bonds to the whims of murder,
> Sprawled in the bowels of the earth,
> The torn fields of France.
> What do you see in our eyes
> At the shrieking iron and flame
> Hurled through still heavens?
> What quaver – what heart aghast?
> Poppies whose roots are in man's veins
> Drop, and are ever dropping;
> But mine in my ear is safe,
> Just a little white with the dust.

The form is free verse. The sense we get of a structure for the poem does not rely on any rhyme scheme or regular scansion of the lines. There is an underlying iambic rhythm, but it is never established for long enough to make that the basis of its coherence. The effect is one of greater spontaneity than Sassoon, though the language is sufficiently mannered in places to create the sense of the poet reflecting on his situation rather than noting his immediate responses. Though not a member of the Imagist group, it is not difficult to see that Rosenberg (1890–1918) had been influenced by their work, and indeed was personally encouraged by Pound.

Most important is Rosenberg's initial concentration on his specific circumstances. The effect of free verse here is to give a far less emotionally wrought image of the trenches than the one we are accustomed to in Sassoon or Owen. It is as though the scene were reduced visually to a neutral depiction of shapes and colours. The rat's indifference to whose hand it touches, English or German, and Rosenberg's reference to 'the whims of murder' lend a note of weary resignation to the poet's awareness of what is happening. It becomes an appropriate rather than a ridiculous gesture for him to 'pull the parapet's poppy/To stick behind my ear.'

The use of free verse here enables us to see how it is a form of writing where a poem is moulded by the progression of the statement being made. The first two lines stand in opposition to each other; the first tells of time passing with the inference of decay in the use of the word 'crumbles':

The dărk-nĕss crŭm-blĕs ă-wáy.

The second claims time as a means of conceiving eternity, and its rhythmic flow is very different, using the regular, more weighty effect of iambics:

Ĭt ĭs thĕ sáme ŏld drú-ĭd tíme ăs év-ĕr

made even more ungainly by the extra short syllable at the end. The sudden movement of the rat is described in a brisk, easily flowing six-syllable line, exactly mirrored by the line which describes the equally sudden movement of the poet placing the poppy behind his ear:

Ă quéer săr-dón-ĭc rát', 'Tŏ stíck bĕ-hínd mў eár.

The poem as a whole has a rhythmical structure beyond the make-up of its individual lines; it is not reliant on a regular framework of scansion, but on a process of managing contrasts and conformities between individual lines and sets of lines.

What makes 'Break of Day in the Trenches' so very different from Sassoon's work is the way in which the poetry is used in the first instance as a mode of *presentation*, rather than as an act of passionate anger and judgement. The whole justification for the composition of 'Suicide in the Trenches' rests in its condemnation of a particular attitude; the judgement is the poem. Rosenberg finishes his poem on what seems a trivial note of detail, the poppy 'Just a little white with dust'. There is very little sense here of a public to be educated in fundamental moral issues. The rat's indifference may suggest that we consider the fighting of 'haughty athletes' in a far less heroic light than was popularly the case at home, but the final four lines deliver an oblique philosophical proposition rather than an angry condemnation. Poppies die, as do men; the red flower is associated with the loss of blood. The poppy Rosenberg has picked will not drop while he protects it, though it is tarnished with dust. The issue is that raised in the first two lines: time as the bringer of decay, juxtaposed to time as the vehicle of eternity.

The war was undoubtedly responsible for a major disruption of continuity in the development of poetry. I.M. Parsons has drawn attention to the way in which poets were forced to consider alternative styles:

> What men and women were experiencing and feeling, after the holocaust of the Somme, if not before, could no longer be given poetic expression by writers whose sensibilities had been conditioned in Edwardian days or earlier, and whose poetic conventions were outworn even before the war started.[9]

The Edwardian poets Parsons is referring to would include Bridges, de la Mare, Hardy, Masefield and W.H. Davies, whose work continued in popularity well after the war, and provided a body of English poetry that established itself as 'traditional' over against the avant-garde work of the Modernists. The poetry of Sassoon and Owen, and to a far lesser degree Rosenberg, soon became known, however, and helped to initiate a degree of change within the dominant traditionalism of the post-war years, as did the publication of the poetry of Gerard Manley Hopkins in 1918 (ironically enough, through the editorship of Bridges). Hopkins's experimentation before the war (he died in 1889) both in rhythm and rhyme, were remarkable enough to influence not just the Modernists of this period; his poetry has had a lasting effect on the evolution of British poetry through to the work of contemporaries like Ted Hughes and Seamus Heaney.

In the 1920s it was Edith Sitwell (1887-1964) as much as the Anglo-American Imagist presence of Pound, Hulme, Aldington, H.D. and Amy Lowell, who was responsible for the first widely publicized reaction against Georgian poetry through her annual anthology, *Wheels*, which ran from 1916 to 1921. It included poetry by Aldous Huxley, and published seven poems by Wilfred Owen in its fourth issue. Sitwell was fascinated by avant-garde developments in the theory of art that had been taking place in Paris since the late nineteenth century. The so-called *Dada-ist* movement (the word, meaning 'hobby-horse', had reputedly been chosen from a dictionary at random) laid the foundations upon which the Surrealists were to build from around 1924. *Dada* owed its inception (*c.*1916) in no small degree to the way in which the war was highlighting the fragmentation of modern society. Its approach was destructive and cynical, breaking down traditional forms and challenging orthodox critical discourse. In the meantime, Pound had moved on from Imagism to embrace Vorticism, a movement

---

[9] I.M. Parsons, *Men Who March Away*, London: Chatto & Windus (1965), p. 14.

founded by Wyndham Lewis, based on the Cubist work of Picasso. Cubism and Surrealism were closely allied, the former requiring the artist to reduce the subject to its basic, simple shapes, often presenting several views of it at once. The juxtaposition of a variety of apparently incongruous images or ideas, implying a fundamental fluidity in terms of their relationships, was effectively a means of portraying the insubstantiality of received notions of social coherence.

It is possible to appreciate why, in the light of this experimentation, English poets were becoming interested once more in the work of seventeenth-century 'Metaphysical' poets, who practised the technique of pursuing surprising and revealing contrasts between object and 'conceit', or image.

The Sitwells, Edith and her two brothers, Osbert and Sacheverell, were closely associated with the Bloomsbury Group, a coterie which centred around Virginia and Leonard Woolf. Virginia Woolf's 'stream of consciousness' technique in her novels was influenced by Surrealist theories of art as an expression of the subconscious mind, where formal restraints were required to be sublimated in order to allow connections and associations to flow from a deeper level. Like the Sitwells, the Bloomsbury Group presented an image of Bohemian contempt for the social and moral constraints of society. Where they differed from Pound was in their development of a response which identified them as essentially English, and still very much a part of the upper-class intelligentsia. Their position, regardless of their interest in European literature, was to be understood in terms of their reaction to English literature: a rejection of Romanticism and its humanist optimism, and of Victorian social realism. In 1925, Virginia Woolf was prepared to argue that while her own mood was one of optimism, it was the optimism of an iconoclast, not a Romantic:

> We are sharply cut off from our predecessors. A shift in the scale – the sudden slip of masses held in position for ages – has shaken the fabric from top to bottom, alienated us from the past and made us perhaps too vividly conscious of the present. Every day we find ourselves doing, saying, or thinking things that would have been impossible to our fathers. And we feel the differences which have not been noted far more keenly than the resemblances which have been very perfectly expressed. New books lure us to read them partly in the hope that they will reflect this rearrangement of our attitude – these scenes, thoughts, and apparently fortuitous groupings of incongruous things which impinge upon us with so keen a sense of novelty – and, as literature does, give it back into our keeping, whole and comprehended. Here indeed there is every reason for optimism.[10]

Like Wilfred Owen, Edith Sitwell was deeply influenced by the poetry of

---

[10]'How It Strikes A Contemporary', in Virginia Woolf, *The Common Reader, First Series*, London: The Hogarth Press (1925), p. 299.

Rimbaud, Mallarmé and Baudelaire. Her view of contemporary civilization remained un-Romantically pessimistic, cynically mocking the spiritual deadness of the times. Her poetry dwelt on the superficialities of life, and to this end she developed a self-consciously eccentric style, emphatically rhythmical and apparently chaotic in its imagery. Like Evelyn Waugh, writing of the manic gaiety of high society in the 20s in *Vile Bodies* (1930), she presented her audience with a cheerful mask behind which there always lurked a sense of despair:

> Look through those periwigged green trees
> At the täll house . . . impressions seize!
>
> Trees periwigged and snuffy; old
> Is silence, with its tales all told,
> And Time is shrunken, bare and cold,
>
> And here the malefactor Death
> Snuffs out the candle with our breath.[11]

In 1923 she wrote and performed *Façade*, poetry recited to music written for it by William Walton. Walton's score now has the effect of a nostalgic look at the popular musical rhythms and harmonic clichés of the 1920s. At the time, however, it was conceived of as part of a satirical comment on the brittle façade maintained by the upper classes in a time of increasing economic uncertainty and depression. In keeping with the spirit of *Façade*, Sitwell herself remained hidden from view as she recited the poetry.

Sitwell and Huxley, in company with D.H. Lawrence and Edgell Rickword, were part of an essentially English Modernist trend. They were helped by a contemporary critical atmosphere which sought to deny the centrality of the Romantic tradition in English literature, and to revive in its place an interest in the seventeenth century. Late nineteenth-century poetry and the work of the Georgians continued to be savagely attacked. T.S. Eliot and Middleton Murry were influential in this respect, joined in 1928 by Robert Graves (1895–1986), who with Laura Riding published in that year *A Survey of Modernist Poetry*, an indication that Graves had moved significantly from his initial traditionalist position.

The Modernist phase in British poetry, generally seen as losing its impetus after 1930, had therefore become a complex phenomenon. Central to it was a reaction against Romanticism, yet the legacy of nineteenth-century poetry was by no means lost. From the Imagist movement on, Modernism had come increasingly to represent a poetry of withdrawal, where Romanticism had insisted on the need for the involvement to some extent of the

---

[11]'The Man With The Green Patch', in Edith Sitwell, *Collected Poems*, London: Macmillan (1957), p. 47. Hereafter *Sitwell*.

poet in contemporary events. The social and political spectre of dissociation and fragmentation had prompted Modernist poets to search for the roots of their art in an alternative context; politically this was inclined to endow the movement with conservative or reactionary tendencies.

Eliot's *The Waste Land* in many respects revealed the major strengths and weaknesses of the movement; the disturbing power of its social critique on the one hand, describing a culturally fruitful land reduced to 'a handful of dust', and on the other, the impossibility of progression for art in that situation. The poem rapidly established itself as a landmark in the development of Modernism; it combines references to the tragic difficulties that were then besetting Eliot in his private life with repeated images of what seemed to him the cultural incoherence of post-war Europe:

> Here is no water but only rock
> Rock and no water and the sandy road
> The road winding above among the mountains
> Which are mountains of rock without water
> If there were water we should stop and drink
> Amongst the rock one cannot stop or think
> Sweat is dry and feet are in the sand
> If there were only water amongst the rock
> Dead mountain mouth of carious teeth that cannot spit
> Here one can neither stand nor lie nor sit
> There is not even silence in the mountains
> But dry sterile thunder without rain
> There is not even solitude in the mountains
> But red sullen faces sneer and snarl
> From doors of mudcracked houses . . .
> ('What the Thunder said' 11. 331-45)

Eliot's quest for order and authority is expressed through allusions to ancient mythologies, specifically the Grail legend with its religious connotations, through Christianity itself in a variety of biblical references, and through allusions to poets who, like Dante, are intended to invoke a quality of 'universality' as it has been in the past. As always, the key to Eliot's main concern is the poet's need to become detached from his subject, 'the poet has not a "personality" to express, but a particular medium'.[12] The poem arguably achieves, with its combined use of Symbolist and Imagist techniques, and its constantly shifting poetic forms, what the Imagists in particular sought: in Michael Schmidt's words, 'He alters our way of reading, if we read him properly. The poem does not respond to analysis of its meanings – meanings cannot be detached from the texture of the poetry itself' (*Schmidt* p. 130). In the final section of the poem there is a degree of

---

[12] *Tradition and the Individual Talent*, in *Eliot S.E.* pp. 19-20.

optimism achieved in the context of the self-denying religious philosophies of the east. Three key words from one of the sacred Hindu texts, the *Upanishads*, dominate the poem's conclusion: *Datta, Dayadhvam*, and *Damyata*; 'give', 'sympathize', and 'control'. The poet must strive to do what society itself can no longer achieve, submit 'To controlling hands':

> *Damyata*: The boat responded
> Gaily, to the hand expert with sail and oar
> The sea was calm, your heart would have responded
> Gaily, when invited, beating obedient
> To controlling hands . . .
> ('What the Thunder said' 11.418–22)

Eliot's personal situation inevitably coloured his Modernist vision of society. He was an exile, trying to discover his roots in English soil while his personal life was, at the time of writing the poem, in a sufficient state of disarray to drive him into a nervous breakdown. The pessimism of *The Wasteland* was by no means typical of the Modernism pursued by Bloomsbury and the Sitwells, but the poem became the most influential text of the movement and existed both as a point of arrival and departure. Eliot had no wish to associate himself directly with what he referred to in 1923 as 'the immense panorama of futility and anarchy which is contemporary history'.[13] His subsequent poetry was to delineate a voyage in search of his personal salvation and sense of identity. The younger poets of the period were prepared to see themselves as part of the new era Virginia Woolf had prophesied was coming. Among these poets was W.H. Auden, who saw in the bleak prospect of the future depicted by Eliot a reason not for withdrawal, but for a change of emphasis, which included recognition of left-wing politics as a potential force for good in society.

Recognizing the importance of Eliot as the poet who had substantially given the lie to the poetic tradition of Wordsworth, and in whose style lay the basis of a way forward, Auden equally insisted on the role of the poet as one deeply involved in society. Edward Mendelson, in the Introduction to his edition of Auden's *Selected Poems* has summed up the reasons why he and many other critics have come to see in Auden 'the first poet writing in English who felt at home in the twentieth century':

> He welcomed into his poetry all the disordered conditions of his time, all its variety of language and event. In this, as in almost everything else, he differed from his modernist predecessors such as Yeats, Lawrence, Eliot or Pound, who had turned nostalgically away from a flawed present to some lost illusory Eden where life was unified,

---

[13]T.S. Eliot, in *The Dial*, 'Ulysses, Order and Myth' (1923), quoted in Stan Smith, *Inviolable Voice: History and Twentieth Century Poetry*, Dublin: Gill & Macmillan (1982), p. 11. Hereafter *Smith*.

hierarchy secure, and the grand style a natural extension of the vernacular. All of this Auden rejected. His continuing subject was the task of the present moment: erotic and political tasks in his early poems, ethical and religious ones later.[14]

---

[14]W.H. Auden, *Selected Poems*, ed. Edward Mendelson, London: Faber & Faber (1979), p. ix. Hereafter *Auden*.

3
Post-Modernist Poetry 1930–1950

The onset of the 1930s marks the beginning of a new phase in twentieth-century British poetry, a dominant feature of which was the rapidly growing reputation of W.H. Auden (1907–74). Three anthologies edited by Michael Roberts contributed materially to Auden's success: *New Signatures* of 1932, *New Country* of 1933, and in 1936, *The Faber Book of Modern Verse*. The poets who comprised a so-called 'Auden group' (including Louis MacNeice, Rex Warner, C. Day Lewis and Stephen Spender) were consequently often referred to collectively as the 'New Country' poets.

In his Preface to *New Country*, Michael Roberts declares the common interest of its contributors:

> If Marxism seems to us to be tainted with its nineteenth-century origin yet nevertheless to be, in the main, true, if, in the hands of its present exponents, the doctrine seems inelastic and fails to understand a temper which is not merely bourgeois but inherently English, it is for us to prepare the way for an English Lenin by modifying and developing that doctrine.[1]

Despite the fact that there presumably should have been a semi-colon after 'true', the point is clear. After Eliot's insistence that the poet should function as a 'catalyst',[2] a disinterested agent, a new generation of poets responded by reasserting their own personal commitment to and involvement in the process of social and political change which seemed paramount at a time of impending dislocation. 'It is essential,' Roberts wrote, 'that intellectuals should become part of the community, not servants of a financial machine, and to do that they must realize that all this time they have been such servants and the measure of their servitude is the measure of the difficulty which they experience in rebelling' (*New Country* p. 15).

It is understandable why, though the 1930s and 40s saw the evolution of

---

[1] *New Country: Prose and Poetry by the authors of New Signatures*, ed. Michael Roberts, London: Hogarth Press (1933), p. 11. Hereafter *New Country*.
[2] *Tradition and the Individual Talent*, in *Eliot S.E.* p. 18.

a 'neo-Romantic' movement often in declared opposition to the New Country poets, some critics have found themselves defining Auden as – to some degree at least – a Romantic (see *Pelican Guide VII* pp. 377–93). Poets like Day Lewis, Spender, MacNeice and Auden felt morally obliged to register a response that was – to recall Arnold's account of why the French Revolution had had a harmful effect on early nineteenth-century poetry – of a 'political, practical character'. In ideological terms, this meant that the break with Modernism could hardly have been more extreme; as Geoffrey Thurley has argued, 'To grow to maturity after the Great War and under the shadow of the Depression and of rising Fascism was sufficient to make acceptance of Marxism practically an intellectual necessity.[3]

Other parallels with the evolution of Romanticism over against the hegemony of Classicism suggest themselves, in particular the use of traditional English rather than Augustan, Latinate poetic forms (the contrast illustrated earlier through Warton and Blake). Auden's rhythms and his use of rhyme and stanza suggest a return to native poetic form, specifically here the recollection of nursery-rhyme doggerel and folk-song:

> O what is that sound which so thrills the ear
>   Down in the valley drumming, drumming?
> Only the scarlet soldiers, dear,
>   The soldiers coming.
>
> O what is that light I see flashing so clear
>   Over the distance brightly, brightly?
> Only the sun on their weapons, dear,
>   As they step lightly.
>
> (*Auden* pp. 26–7)

As with many nursery-rhymes, the juxtaposition of ingenuous form and sinister content creates a disturbing, haunting effect in these lines, all the more effective for its associations with the intimacy of much children's poetry. If we compare 'O what is that sound' with T.S. Eliot's 'The Hippopotamus' or 'Sweeney Among the Nightingales', where a regularly scanned and rhymed four-line verse pattern is applied to a very different order of subject, it serves to emphasize how Auden was turning with a new approach to the medium to capture the immediacy which the properties of the traditional folk-song could yield. Eliot, on the other hand, continued to express a 'Modernist' sense of aloofness, and lack of contact with anything like a collective 'folk' consciousness in the contemporary world.

The New Country poets belonged like the major Romantic poets before them (excepting Blake) to a priveleged minority within society. Both sets of poets were to find themselves trying to reach across the gap which divided them from a section of society with which they wished to identify and in

---

[3]Geoffrey Thurley, *The Ironic Harvest*, London: Edward Arnold (1974), p. 62. Hereafter *Thurley*.

some measure represent, but which they also feared as a potentially destructive force. One of the most distinctive features of Auden's poetry in the 30s is its confessional quality, repeatedly expressing a class-guilt made all the more agonizing by the honesty with which he admits that he is reluctant to lose the comforts of privilege, 'The leisured drives through a land of farms':

> Lucky, this point in time and space
> Is chosen as my working place;
>   Where the sexy airs of summer,
> The bathing hours and the bare arms,
> The leisured drives through a land of farms,
>   Are good to the newcomer.
>
> Equal with colleagues in a ring
> I sit on each calm evening,
>   Enchanted as the flowers
> The opening light draws out of hiding
> From leaves with all its dove-like pleading
>   Its logic and its powers.
> ('Out on the lawn I lie in bed' *Auden* pp. 29–32)

As a number of critics have observed, 'luck' and 'lucky' are words which occur regularly in Auden's poetry. The cumulative effect of this is that luck comes to mean more than mere chance, it signifies something in the nature of a gift not to be lightly parted with. The luck of a luxurious life surrounded by a small coterie of intellectual friends cannot go unchallenged, however:

> The creepered wall stands up to hide
> The gathering multitudes outside
>   Whose glances hunger worsens;
> Concealing from their wretchedness
> Our metaphysical distress,
>   Our kindness to ten persons.
>
> Soon through the dykes of our content
> The crumpling flood will force a rent,
>   And, taller than a tree,
> Hold sudden death before our eyes
> Whose river-dreams long hid the size
>   And vigours of the sea.

Wordsworth, confronted by the revolutionary political actions and ideas of his time, but excluded from them to a significant degree by the nature of his background and education, was soon forced to abandon the generalized rhetoric of eighteenth-century sentimental poetry in favour of an almost obsessively personalized analysis of his own state of mind and motives for action. The poets of the Auden group appear to have reacted to their situation in a similar way. By no means all the New Country poets confessed to the uncertainties Auden was prepared to reveal, but central to the effect they sought was the understanding that it was the poet in person who addressed the reader from the page. Encouraging everyone to undertake a session of honest self-appraisal became a recurring theme in much of the poetry, as here in this extract from C. Day Lewis's *The Magnetic Mountain*:

> The man with his tongue in his cheek, the woman
> With her heart in the wrong place, unhandsome, unwholesome;
> Have exposed the new-born to worse than weather,
> Exiled the honest and sacked the seer.
> These drowned the farms to form a pleasure-lake,
> In time of drought they drain the reservoir
> Through private pipes for baths and sprinklers.[4]

This stands in marked contrast to what Eliot had been striving to achieve in *The Waste Land* where, despite its narrative discontinuities, the dominant voice is intended to be that of the Theban soothsayer, Tiresias, 'old man with wrinkled dugs'.[5] In Book III of *Metamorphosis*, Ovid (43 BC – AD 17) describes Tiresias as so wise that death could not quench his wisdom, and further tells the story of how he spent part of his life changed into a woman. It is significant that in his note in *The Waste Land* on Tiresias, Eliot italicizes the word 'sees', when discussing 'What Tiresias *sees*'. The soothsayer had been struck blind by Juno; what he sees is not the immediate everyday world, but a vision of the future granted to him by Jupiter. Tiresias is Eliot's attempt to sink his own individualism in a timeless, sexually ambivalent persona. When we compare this with the self-revelatory, confessional mode so characteristic of Auden and Day Lewis, it is by no means irrelevant to think also of the way Wordsworth, often picturing himself in the company of a small group of like-minded friends, repeatedly takes a central part in his own poetry in order to draw attention to the inadequacy of his judgement when dominated by the conventions of an older generation.

In broad terms, therefore, the period between 1930 and the outbreak of the Second World War does have certain features in common with the period which produced the Romantic Movement in England some 150 years before. For those who disapproved of what Wordsworth was doing at

---

[4]*Poetry of the Thirties*, ed. Robin Skelton, Penguin Books (1964), p. 61. Hereafter *Skelton*.
[5]Section III: 'The Fire Sermon' 1.228.

the turn of the eighteenth century, the 1790s produced a breed of 'Jacobin', or politically subversive, poets. In the early 1940s, F.R. Leavis referred with similar distaste to the 1930s as a 'Marxizing decade'.[6] The political climate since the First World War had gradually established an increasingly intrusive effect on the work of many poets, to a point where some kind of break with the immediate past was evidently taking place. The fact that a similar deepening of political awareness allied to a more or less radical reassessment of society took place at the end of the eighteenth century may help to explain why the early Romantics began to enjoy something of a revival in the 1930s. The association of Modernism with a critique of Romanticism and the rediscovery, through Pound and the Imagists, of the virtues of Classicism, further encourages the idea that the attack on Modernism signifies a renewed spirit of Romanticism.

Acting to some extent as a counterpoint to the political context, is a literary context which for both the early Romantics and the poets of the 30s meant that a sense of continuity with the immediate past remained important. In the case of the New Country poets we are given a reminder of this in the anecdote of Auden reputedly announcing to Neville Coghill, his tutor at Oxford, that he had torn up all his poems 'Because they are no good. Based on Wordsworth', adding, 'I've been reading Eliot. I now see the way I want to write' (*Pinto* p. 173). For Auden's generation, Eliot remained unquestionably the major poet of the day, and if it is important to identify the way in which 30s poetry marks a break with Modernism, it is equally important to identify the continuing influence of Eliot. One quality often assigned to Auden has been that he was an 'intellectual' poet, and the eclipse of Wordsworth by the discovery of Eliot denotes his admiration for the way Eliot filtered his emotional responses through a highly trained, erudite mind. It was to Eliot, then a director at Faber & Faber, that Auden sent his early poems, and it was Eliot who eventually published Auden's first collection in 1930. From the outset, Eliot was well aware that Auden's promise pointed in directions different from those which his own work had taken, but he actively encouraged Auden, Spender and MacNeice, and subsequently George Barker and Vernon Watkins.

The most obvious way in which Auden sought at first to emulate Eliot emerges in his severe use of language, pruning words from sentences to leave little more than a skeletal form, often more suggestive of profundity than actually profound:

> To ask the hard question is simple;
> Asking at meeting
> With the simple glance of acquaintance
> To what these go

[6]'Literature and Society' in *The Common Pursuit*, London: Chatto & Windus (1952), p. 182. Hereafter *L.S.*

> And how these do:
> To ask the hard question is simple,
> The simple act of the confused will.
> *(Auden, p. 17)*

The guru-like persona behind these incantatory lines is reminiscent of Eliot's 'Gerontion' (1920), an old man uttering 'Thoughts of a dry brain in a dry season', but it is surely *Prufrock* that Auden has particularly in mind:

> To lead you to an overwhelming question . . .
> Oh, do not ask, 'What is it?'
> Let us go and make our visit.

Stylistic borrowing of this nature was relatively short lived; Auden has established himself in retrospect as a poet not of any single, predominating style, but rather as a poet capable of turning his hand to a wide range of metrical and rhetorical forms. At a deeper level, his admiration for Eliot's work arguably stemmed from the fact that he could find there an intellectually convincing confession of faith in an ideal order which he recognized as a confirmation of his own underlying wish to preserve rather than reorder society. In Eliot's case, an intellectual recognition of the power of religion (evident in *The Waste Land* as a symbolic collage of Christianity and Eastern mysticism) turned in due course towards specific Christian commitment. His Modernist belief in 'culture' and 'art' as a self-sufficient medium 'capable of embodying and communicating its own values' (*Ackroyd* p. 239) in opposition to the Romantic tradition of striving to reconcile art and society, was abandoned in favour of an appeal to the overriding, healing power of the Christian faith:

> Suffer us not to mock ourselves with falsehood
> Teach us to care and not to care
> Teach us to sit still
> Even among these rocks,
> Our peace in His will
> And even among these rocks
> Sister, mother
> And spirit of the river, spirit of the sea,
> Suffer me not to be separated
>
> And let my cry come unto Thee.
> *(Ash-Wednesday* (1930) Section VI 11.26–35)

Eliot, Peter Ackroyd argues, 'helped to create the idea of a modern movement with his own "difficult" poetry, and then assisted at its burial' (*Ackroyd* p. 239). The major work of Eliot's later years was *Four Quartets*

(1935-1942), a series of meditative poems in which the primacy of man's search for spirituality calls into question all notions of historical determinism, and in particular our enthusiasm for temporal and essentially transient beliefs grounded in present political circumstances. The belief that history reveals a 'pattern' and is more than 'mere sequence' is:

> ... a partial fallacy
> Encouraged by superficial notions of evolution,
> Which becomes, in the popular mind, a means of disowning the past.
> ('The Dry Salvages' Section II 11.39-41)

It is with phrases like 'the popular mind' that Eliot revealed an attitude so difficult for Auden's generation to accept, looking as they were for a poetic voice which would engage with a world 'dominated by economic depression, the rise of fascism, and rumours of wars' (*Smith* p. 128-9). Auden's poem 'Out on the lawn I lie in bed' has already illustrated that it was still difficult to escape from the culturally and socially defined position of the poet for whom history, as Stan Smith has argued, was 'a fossilized and alien force ... influential in denying, thwarting, suppressing all the self's movements to freedom and fulfilment' (*Smith* p. 21-2).

In *Four Quartets* Eliot was effectively using his own religious faith to make his peace with history, thereby liberating the self of which he had been so suspicious in its Romantic, humanist manifestations:

> ... This is the use of memory:
> For liberation — not less of love but expanding
> Of love beyond desire, and so liberation
> From the future as well as the past. Thus, love of a country
> Begins as attachment to our own field of action
> And comes to find that action of little importance
> Though never indifferent. History may be servitude,
> History may be freedom. See, now they vanish,
> The faces and places, with the self which, as it could, loved them,
> To become renewed, transfigured, in another pattern.
> ('Little Gidding' Section III 11.7-16)

Smith goes on to argue that the Auden group were unable to make any significant break with what, as a Marxist, he understands to be a firmly rooted class view of history, with 'its origins in the objective conditions in which the English intelligentsia came to consciousness, at the centre of an Empire ... and cushioned from global crisis by layers of imperial fat' (*Smith* p. 18).

Most critics are agreed that for all their sense of a need to inhabit the historical world of current events, the Auden group in the 30s only ever operated within the context of the intellectual ambiance of their own social world. The changes wrought profoundly affected the writing of poetry within that traditional ambiance, but never succeeded in breaking down the traditional, cultural pattern of relationships between poet and readership. The material testing ground for the intellectual commitment of the Marxist poets of this decade came with the Spanish Civil War, and its effect was – almost without exception – to disillusion them:

> The Communists appeared more intent upon the destruction of the Anarchists and Trotskyites than on that of the Fascists, and it was clear that, far from being a struggle for democratic liberties, the civil war had become a military training ground for the Axis powers, and a pageant of propaganda for the Communists. (*Skelton* p. 19)

Auden himself departed for America early in 1939, jettisoning his belief in Marxism for Christianity, a path which inevitably provokes some further degree of comparison with the course taken by the disillusioned Wordsworth in the aftermath of the French Revolution.

To identify the pervasive qualities of 'the first poet writing in English who felt at home in the twentieth century' involves, therefore, the recognition of a number of contradictory influences on him. We will best understand the extent to which his poetry is innovatory if we relate his work to the literary rather than the political or sociological context of the time. Geoffrey Thurley, for example, has argued that Auden – despite an antagonistic Marxist phase – belongs no less surely with the mainstream of English poetry up to 1930, even if those critically defining it at the time – notably F.R. Leavis in *New Bearings in English Poetry* (1932) – had no intention of placing him alongside Hopkins, Pound and Eliot: 'For Auden, as for Leavis,' Thurley concludes, 'self-knowledge is the chief end of poetry' (*Thurley* p. 54).

In *New Bearings* Leavis continued the attack on nineteenth-century Romanticism begun by the Imagists and developed by Eliot in his literary criticism. The 'great' Romantics – Wordsworth, Coleridge, Byron, Shelley and Keats – are worthy of admiration but flawed. Subsequent uncritical admiration for the Romantics, however, meant that 'Wit, play of intellect, stress of cerebral muscle had no place ...' in nineteenth-century poetry.[7] Leavis argued forcibly on behalf of the interrelatedness of literature and society, but against the Marxist 'materialist interpretation' of society based on economic theory (*L.S.* p. 185). Before the Romantic Movement came to encourage poets that 'the actual world is alien, recalcitrant and unpoetical' (*New Bearings* p. 15), the proposition that man was both an individual and a social being was workable, workable essentially because the concept of an intelligentsia capable of registering the relationship between literature and society was recognized. Where Marxist

---

[7] F.R. Leavis, *New Bearings in English Poetry*, London: Chatto & Windus (1932), p. 9. Hereafter *New Bearings*.

philosophy, with its 'economic and material determinants' (*L.S.* p. 184) is hostile to notions of an intelligentsia, a theory of society which recognizes 'intellectual and spiritual' determinants is not (*L.S.* p. 184).

Leavis's criticism illustrates how the debate revolving around twentieth-century poetry continued to be a debate relating to the nature and consequences of the Romantic Movement in England. The issue is one of how the poetic voice relates to society, of the 'individual talent' and its understanding of the 'historical forces' which give it 'birth, occasion and pretext' (*Smith* p. 20). The political ambivalence of Auden's Marxist poetry, registering his individualistic response to collective solutions, identifies his work as a record of this debate in continuing process; his 'position', however, is never made clear. The language makes all-embracing gestures of colloquialism, while at the same time operating within the cultural idioms of public school life, especially the sporting variety:

> You're thinking us a nasty sight;
> Yes, we are poisoned, you are right,
> > Not even clean;
> We do not know how to behave
> We are not beautiful or brave
> You would not pick our sort to save
> > Your first fifteen.
> ('A Communist to Others' *Skelton* p. 55)

In reaction to Modernism he abandoned Eliot's attempt at a neutral, Tiresian voice to replace it with verse forms and idioms which only resulted in an alternative kind of exclusiveness. The coterie atmosphere of Auden's poetry with its in-jokes has long been a bone of critical contention. Both the English landscape in a specifically visual sense, and the climate of feeling it embodied for Auden's contemporaries are made startlingly real in his verse, in a way they are not in Eliot's scholarly caricaturing of London life in *The Waste Land*; yet the force of his imagery – for all its apparent particularity – makes itself felt through his ability to generalize, as in the following lines:

> I see barns falling, fences broken,
> Pasture not ploughland, weeds not wheat.
> The great houses remain but only half are inhabited,
> Dusty the gunrooms and the stable clocks stationary.
> Some have been turned into prep-schools where the diet is in the
> > hands of an experienced matron,
> Others into club-houses for the golf-bore and the top-hole.
> > ('The Summer holds: upon its glittering lake' *Auden* p. 37)

Auden's admiration for Wilfred Owen is worth recalling here; as with Owen, the manner of observation guarantees no direct confrontation with specific political issues arising from the images. The result is atmospheric rather than concrete.

The latter part of 'The Summer Holds' (1932?-4), written in a contrastingly taut rhythmic and rhyming form, counters the Georgian sense of regret for the passing of an era when the aristocracy maintained the social and aesthetic order of society, with the threat of change through revolutionary action. But it remains politically as vague as the first section of the poem. Precisely who will constitute the revolutionary force remains undefined. Auden's description of the middle and lower orders of society in the first section suggests more of an aristocratic disdain for them than a comradely affection on his part:

> . . . another population, with views about nature,
> Brought in charabanc and saloon along arterial roads;
> Tourists to whom the Tudor cafés
> Offer Bovril and buns upon Breton ware
> With leather-work as a sideline . . .

To the extent that Auden was, as Thurley claims, primarily motivated as a poet by his quest for self-knowledge, he does indeed appear to retain close affinities with the early Romantics. Like them, his work evolved initially from a sense of personal identity defined in the context of a small circle of friends and family, not of society as a national concept. The extent to which this could continually undermine his New Country, Marxist, 'collective' persona is evident in the fascination which theories of psychoanalysis held for him.

From the outset, poets of Auden's generation reflected the current interest in the work of Freud, and his theories of the subconscious mind. Auden's poetry was influenced throughout by the jargon of psychoanalysis, a field of study which emphasized individual motivation in relation to society and was therefore fundamentally at odds with Marxist philosophy. In the 30s, however, the two were often yoked together to the extent that, as Robin Skelton has commented, for 'some revolutionaries, it seemed that, though Marx was God, Freud was his prophet' (*Skelton* pp. 30-1). The influence of psychoanalysis on Auden's poetry is not, however, of primary significance when one considers his influence on later poets. Far more telling was his return to the rhythms and rhymes of traditional English poetry, and his use of conventional, if often startling, imagery. The effect he ultimately achieved was a tone of ironic urbanity, setting aside the eternal, cosmic and theological matters of significance pursued by Eliot, bringing to the fore in their place a confused, self-mocking poet who observed his social environment, and made poetry of it by a subtle process of defamiliarization.

The saving grace of the human condition for Auden became love, a quality perceived as mysteriously surviving in the world while being not of it. This conviction surfaces in his poetry throughout the 1930s. In 1934 he wrote:

> Yours is the choice, to whom the gods awarded
> The language of learning and the language of love,
> Crooked to move as a moneybug or a cancer
>   Or straight as a dove.
>   ('Easily, my dear, you move . . .' *Auden* p. 36)

After his voluntary exile to the United States it became the dominant antidote to human muddle and tragedy, emphasizing the way in which specifically Christian themes were beginning to influence his writing.

'September 1, 1939' is an excellent illustration of Auden's down-beat manner. The three heavy stresses of each line combine with the language and setting to evoke the musical idiom of the 'blues'. The image with which the poem begins is also redolent of the way America actively visualized itself (through film and photography as well as visual art) in the 1930s:

> I sit in one of the dives
> On Fifty-Second Street
> Uncertain and afraid
> As the clever hopes expire
> Of a low dishonest decade . . .
>   (*Auden* p. 86)

Auden returned repeatedly to the theme of the modern city as dehumanizing; here he combines that with his own sense of having ducked the political issue, only to counter the charge with an ironic dismissal of the 'euphoric dream'. New York is a place of limbo, inhabited throughout by exiles of every nationality, a Babel where 'Each language pours its vain/Competitive excuse'.

From this poem there emerges the voice of a man sounding genuinely disoriented by the loss of ideals that had sustained him to that point; in this respect we might compare the mood of the poem to that of the passage already quoted from Wordsworth's *Home at Grasmere*. What he is left with is his 'voice', the voice with which he must somehow make known his conviction that there remains hope. 'All I have is a voice/To undo the folded lie . . .' It is as though language may be folded like the paper upon which it is written, distorting its appearance; communication is hazardous even when no harm is intended:

> Defenceless under the night
> Our world in stupor lies;
> Yet, dotted everywhere,
> Ironic points of light

> Flash out wherever the Just
> Exchange their messages:
> May I, composed like them
> Of Eros and of dust,
> Beleaguered by the same
> Negation and despair,
> Show an affirming flame.

The messages of the 'Just' are recognizable by their irony; none is exempt from the 'Negation and despair' of life, but the 'Ironic . . . light' will both prevent us from believing a materialistic 'euphoric dream', and free us to 'Show an affirming flame'. At the end of the penultimate verse he restates his conviction already noted from the poem 'Easily, my dear, you move . . .': 'We must love one another or die.'

The difficulty that often arises when looking for Audenesque influences on other poems remains Auden's own remarkable range of poetic voice. 'At the Grave of Henry James' (1941) is an elegy on the American novelist, Henry James, written in a carefully controlled yet relaxed and meditative stanza form. The imagery is at once immediate and beautifully realized, yet highly complex. With James as his focal point, Auden chose to celebrate the virtues of a meticulous writer characterized as 'Master of nuance and scruple', committed to his art of portraying the minutiae of human relationships, and not swayed by the 'brilliant uproar' of larger historic events. This is Auden writing with a far more formal voice than that chosen for the other poems so far quoted, yet he is still able seemingly to throw lines away as though something approaching slang will do. What is Audenesque about this is the artistry with which it is done; the style may at times seem unpremeditated, but the effect is always the result of his own carefully contrived concern for 'nuance and scruple':

> The snow, less intransigent than their marble,
> Has left the defence of whiteness to these tombs;
>   For all the pools at my feet
> Accommodate blue now, and echo such clouds as occur
> To the sky, and whatever bird or mourner the passing
>   Moment remarks they repeat
>
> While the rocks, named after singular spaces
> Within which images wandered once that caused
>   All to tremble and offend,
> Stand here in an innocent stillness, each marking the spot
> Where one more series of errors lost its uniqueness
>   And novelty came to an end.

> To whose real advantage were such transactions
> When words of reflection were exchanged for trees?
>   What living occasion can
> Be just to the absent? O noon but reflects on itself,
> And the small taciturn stone that is the only witness
>   To a great and talkative man
>
> Has no more judgement than my ignorant shadow
> Of odious comparisons or distant clocks
>   Which challenge and interfere
> With the heart's instantaneous reading of time, time that is
> A warm enigma no longer in you for whom I
>   Surrender my private cheer.
>   (*Auden*, verses I–IV p. 119)

Two qualities are identified in the first verse. The intransigent permanence of the marble gravestones, associated with death, a quality to be 'defended'; and the transience of the natural world, of life. The snow turns to puddles of water, and the puddles reflect ('echo') what passes. The word 'echo' implies an association of the puddles with words, the inference from the final three lines of verse one being that reflections cannot be a guide to sound judgement; they can do no more than 'repeat' whatever happens, regardless of its worth.

The function of the 'rocks' in verse two (a movement from the contrived function of the gravestones to their essential nature) is to commemorate once living beings, who while they were alive were, like the puddles, influenced by immediate circumstances. Auden's own position as a poet who now reflects very different views from those previously held is implied. Life is summed up as a 'series of errors', influenced by 'novelty' until the point of death.

The third verse asks how the living, so untrustworthy, can hope to judge the dead. They do so in terms of the present, possessed of a fallacious understanding of history. In verse fourteen he writes:

> Then remember me that I may remember
> The test we have to learn to shudder for is not
>   An historical event,
> That neither the low democracy of a nightmare nor
> An army's primitive tidiness may deceive me
>   About our predicament . . .

The stone itself passes no judgement, it has no 'reflection' to offer, it stands in opposition to 'odious comparisons' and the passage of worldly time suggested by 'distant clocks'. The 'heart's instantaneous reading of time' suggests a quality of stillness where true wisdom comes with the intransigence of death, not the perpetual movement of life.

As a writer, he finds himself petitioning for the gift of death, raising the language of the final verses to a point where we catch more than a glimpse of the Eliot of *Four Quartets*:

> All will be judged. Master of nuance and scruple,
> Pray for me and for all writers living or dead;
>   Because there are many whose works
> Are in better taste than their lives; because there is no end
> To the vanity of our calling: make intercession
>   For the treason of all clerks.
>   (Verse XXIII)

There is of course a wry debunking of the status of the writer here in Auden's use of the word 'clerk'.

As with *September 1, 1939*, the theme of the untrustworthiness of language is at the heart of the poem, and the complexity and untrustworthiness of the relationship between writer and artifact is admitted. In death we find our faith, a purpose beyond our own worldly failings and those of an undiscerning populace.

Though the Auden group tends to be seen as the dominant influence on poetry in the 1930s, any such impression must be carefully qualified. Contemporary poets ill at ease with *New Country* Marxist posturing – 'Come then, companions. This is the spring of blood,/heart's hey-day, movement of masses, beginning of good' – deplored the growth of a narrowly Marxist, materialistic school of poetry, trampling underfoot the imaginative and intuitive gifts traditionally associated with poetic inspiration.[8] Among those most to be blamed were Geoffrey Grigson, editor of the critical journal, *New Verse*, and those who contributed to it. *New Verse* not infrequently criticized the New Country poets, but it gave their work and ideas publicity and a general aura of social significance, while Grigson himself maintained an ascerbic defence of Classicism, and made a point of attacking the Sitwells and Bloomsbury. G.S. Fraser, an inveterate enemy of *New Country*, insisted that Auden and his disciples slavishly wrote from 'a false objectivism, a tendency to create pseudo-scientific systems of politics, ethics, theology . . .'[9] On the basis of Auden's *New Country* poems it is possible to sympathize with this view; a line such as 'Like a sea-god the communist orator lands at the pier' may well suggest that the sun was indeed setting on the beauties of English lyric verse. ('Poem' in *New Country* p. 214).

In the late 30s and 40s a self-consciously 'Romantic' revival took place, in

---

[8] Rex Warner, 'Hymn' in *Skelton* pp. 59–61.
[9] Quoted in Linda M. Shires, *British Poetry of the Second World War*, London: Macmillan (1985) p. 37. Hereafter *Shires*.

no small degree as a reaction against the New Country poets. The brief reading of Auden undertaken here, however, will have indicated that his work shows him to be considerably more than merely a representative voice of a 'group', however it be defined. Auden's ambivalence when it came to his political convictions reminds us of the diversity which may exist within any group of artists, and in many respects the New Country poets were part of a larger movement within twentieth-century poetry which can still helpfully be conceived of as Romantic. The new Romantics of the late 30s proved to be similarly diverse; what they had in common was a sense of close identification with the Surrealist movement. General political disenchantment, the increasing inevitability of a second world war, and the religious revival that accompanied this threat encouraged the belief, as Linda M. Shires has written, that politics lay 'outside the realm of poetry; the private individual imagination was more important than any collective myth kit' (*Shires* p. 26).

David Gascoygne had been primarily responsible for reintroducing the Surrealists into Britain in the mid 1930s. He adopted Surrealist techniques in his own poetry, and wrote *A Short Survey of Surrealism* (1935), bringing the work of Éluard and Bréton before the reading public in translation. Surrealism's attempt to follow the apparent vagaries of the subconscious mind, mapping out a world which defied the order imposed upon it by conventional, social and political forces is illustrated in Gascoygne's 'The Very Image':

> An image of an aeroplane
> the propeller is rashers of bacon
> the wings are of reinforced lard
> the tail is made of paper-clips
> the pilot is a wasp
> (*Skelton* pp. 234-5)

Gascoygne's work was eloquently supported by the theoretical writings of Herbert Read (1893-1968):

June, 1936. After a winter long drawn out into bitterness and petulance, a month of torrid heat, of sudden efflorescence, of clarifying storms. In this same month the International Surrealist Exhibition broke over London, electrifying the dry intellectual atmosphere, stirring our sluggish minds to wonder, enchantment and derision. The press, unable to appreciate the significance of a movement of such unfamiliar features, prepared an armoury of mockery, sneers and insults. The duller desiccated weeklies, no less impelled to anticipate the event, commissioned their polyglot gossips, their blasé globetrotters, their old-boy-scouts, to adopt their usual pose of I know all, don't be taken in, there's nothing new under the sun – a pose which merely reflected the general lack of intellectual curiosity in this country.[10]

Read's contribution, primarily as a critic rather than a poet, was central, and his essay *Surrealism and the Romantic Principle* is a seminal document for the study of poetry between the wars.

With a brief apology that what he was concerned with might be deemed a dead issue in the twentieth century, Read resurrected and painstakingly developed the concept of a Classical/Romantic dichotomy both in the arts and in society. His verdict was that an either/or division within the arts was fallacious; his conclusion was Blakean:

> There is a principle of life, of creation, of liberation, and that is the romantic spirit; there is a principle of order, of control and of repression, and that is the classical spirit. . . . Classicism, let it be stated without further preface, represents for us now, and has always represented, the forces of oppression. Classicism is the intellectual counterpart of political tyranny. It was so in the ancient world and in the medieval empires; it was renewed to express the dictatorships of the Renaissance and has ever since been the official creed of capitalism. Wherever the blood of martyrs stains the ground, there you will find a doric column or perhaps a statue of Minerva.
>
> (*Surrealism* pp. 248–9)

The creative artist must inevitably find himself at odds with the governing principles of society; he will become, clinically speaking, a neurotic. Yet Read recognized the impossibility of a totally individualist position, and this is where he wished to distance himself from European Surrealism:

> It may be as well to forestall at once the criticism that . . . the artist is merely the individualist in conflict with society. To a certain extent . . . this is true . . . But his whole effort is directed towards a reconciliation with society, and what he offers to society is not a bagful of his own tricks, his idiosyncracies, but rather some knowledge of the secrets to which he has had access, the secrets of the self which are buried in every man alike, but which only the sensibility of the artist can reveal to us in all their actuality. This 'self' is not the personal possession we imagine it to be; it is largely made up of elements from the unconscious, and the more we learn about the unconscious, the more collective it appears to be. . . . But whereas the universal truths of classicism may be merely the temporal prejudices of an epoch, the universal truths of romanticism are coeval with the evolving consciousness of mankind.
>
> (*Surrealism* p. 250)

---

[10] Herbert Read, *Surrealism and the Romantic Principle* (1936), edited by the author, in *Selected Writings of Sir Herbert Read*, London: Faber & Faber (1963), pp. 246–82. Quote p. 246. Hereafter *Surrealism*.

Read effectively redefinied the concept of Culture offered by Eliot, and subsequently Leavis, in Freudian terms; Culture becomes the 'collective unconscious'. Consequently he rejects also the conformist 'political concept of art' associated with the New Country poets. It is to Wordsworth, Shelley, Byron and Coleridge that he turns in order to find 'the primacy of the imagination' at work (*Surrealism* pp. 250, 267).

Interest in the English Romantic Movement as well as in sixteenth and seventeenth-century literature had been growing steadily since the First World War, when it was not uncommon to find slim volumes of Wordsworth's patriotic poems reprinted as timely encouragement.[11] Ernest de Selincourt pioneered research on *The Prelude*, piecing together the early 1805 text of the poem and publishing it in 1928. A less expensive edition was produced in 1933. This indicates the direction interest in the Romantics was taking. Wordsworth's 'major' work was no longer the tortuous public, philosophical poem, *The Excursion*, but his extended autobiographical work of self-analysis. Investigating the mind of a poet was understandably attractive to a generation now pursuing the application of Freudian theories of the mind to literary appreciation. The Romantics, concerned variously with visionary power, dreams and spontaneity, were recognized as having been misunderstood since at least the time when Arnold's criticisms had begun to gain ground.

As a Freudian, Read's approach was to psychoanalyse his subject. In his essay of 1936, *In Defence of Shelley*,[12] he based his reading of the poetry on his claim that Shelley was a neurotic, a man inescapably at odds with the dominant political and religious *mores* of society. Before this in 1930, he had published a study of Wordsworth, angering many critics by the emphasis he placed on the poet's unhappy early love affair with Annette Vallon in order to explain analytically the falling off of the poet's inspiration in his later work. Great emphasis was placed on the fresh light shed by the earlier, less contrived text of *The Prelude* made available by de Selincourt.

Throughout, Read was insistent on the relevance of renewed studies in Romanticism for the present time. Wordsworth's philosophy, he writes, 'is a noble philosophy':

> ... and because it was fashioned in an age of disillusionment, and in a mood of almost hopeless despair, it is a philosophy that has a particular significance for our own age. For out of a slough of despond, induced by the failure of revolutionary hopes, the bitterness

---

[11] For example, *The Patriotic Poetry of William Wordsworth*, ed. Right Hon. Arthur H.D. Acland, Oxford: Clarendon Press (1915). Acland writes: 'It is of real service to us to have a reminder, in this splendid form, that a dogged and united determination to hold on at whatever cost and if need be for years together, without letting the heart droop or fail, must lead in the end to victory.' p. 5.
[12] Herbert Read, *In Defence of Shelley*, in *Selected Writings op. cit.* note 10 Chapter 3, pp. 150-97. Hereafter *Shelley*.

of personal remorse and self-distrust, Wordsworth plucked a faith of renovation, of new hope, based on a deep insight into transcendental forces which continually operate to transform the world, to bring it in infinite cycles of time a little nearer to the image of God.[13]

In a world threatened once more with the chaos of war, the primary culprit is the spirit of conformity through which contemporary societies have evolved:

> Nothing is simpler to demonstrate than the dependency, in every age, of the official codes of morality on the class interests of those who possess the economic power. The only individuals who protest against injustices – or who make their protest vocal – are in effect the poets and artists of each age, who to the extent that they rely on their imaginative capacities and powers, despise and reject the acquisitive materialism of men of action.
>
> (*Surrealism* p. 255)

The discussion operates, therefore, within an unavoidably political context. Romanticism continually seeks to break down the formalizing, collective 'classical' urge within society. To read poetry with an analytical eye only for 'form' consequently represents a dangerous error, an error of the kind already established at Cambridge by Read's contemporary, I.A. Richards. Taking Wordsworth as his subject, Read writes, 'form is not necessarily an external code. All expression has form: emotion dictates its own rhythm, and rhythm is form. Yet a fixed form is external and that is why more formal types of poetry tend to be classical' (*Wordsworth* p. 171).

Behind contemporary Surrealism, therefore, lie the principles made manifest in the work of the great English Romantics, for whom 'morality is based on liberty and love.' Writing of the Romantic artist who exists potentially in all eras, Read claims that:

> He sees no reason why the frailties of the human race should be erected into a doctrine of original sin, but he realizes that most men are born imperfect and are made less perfect still by their circumstances. Such evils and imperfections cannot wholly be eradicated in any conceivable span of human development. But it is his belief that the whole system of organized control and repression which is the social aspect of present-day morality is psychologically misconceived and positively harmful. He believes, that is to say, in the fullest possible liberation of the impulses and is convinced that what law and oppression have failed to achieve will in due time be brought about by love and fraternity.
>
> (*Surrealism* pp. 281–2)

Politically, Read himself was an anarchist, and the way his literary

---

[13] Herbert Read, *Wordsworth*, London: Faber & Faber (1955), p. 188. Hereafter *Wordsworth*.

criticism was evidently a means of presenting anarchist propaganda laid him open to attack from the outset. Despite this his influence on poetry between the wars was considerable, in particular with respect to his championship of a British school of Surrealism. He was by no means alone in offering an alternative to the Marxist critique of society associated with the Auden group. The intellectual ground for a Romantic revival was prepared not only by Read and de Selincourt, but by the literary criticism of C.S. Lewis, Sir Geoffrey Keynes, Mona Wilson, Kathleen Raine and Helen Darbishire, with American critics – among them S. Foster Damon, Arthur Beatty and R.D. Havens – making a significant contribution. Equally important in this respect were the novels and poetry of Charles Williams, steeped in mysticism and the occult, and the work of Dorothy Sayers. It was Read in particular, however, who was responsible for emphasizing potentially radical implications of the new Romanticism through his repeated criticism of the power structures of modern capitalist societies.

Our reading of this period since the mid 1950s has arguably been distorted through the critical position established by Robert Conquest, who published an anthology entitled *New Lines* in 1956. Building his collection of poems primarily around the new and exciting talent of Philip Larkin (1922-86), Conquest delivered a seething attack on 1940s Romanticism. The *New Lines* poets were subsequently given the collective title of The Movement, and the *New Lines* Introduction came to acquire the status of a Movement manifesto. In that Introduction, Conquest criticized 'the sort of corruption which has affected the general attitude to poetry in the last decade'. Poets of the 1940s 'were encouraged to produce diffuse and sentimental verbiage, or hollow technical pirouettes'.[14] Conquest himself is not prepared to do much more than lament in general terms what he calls the rapid collapse of public taste'. The assumption is, of course, that Conquest knows what 'good taste' is; but he stops short at pointing the finger of derision at people who actually like to have china ducks winging their way across the sitting-room wall. Something of that assumption of superiority does find its way into the Introduction, however, by way of using Aldous Huxley as the front man. He is quoted – it must be said with qualified approval – inveighing against 'the sort of people whose bowels yearn at the disgusting caterwaulings of Tziganes; who love to listen to Negroes and Cossacks; who swoon at the noises of the Hawaiian guitar, the Russian balalaika, the Argentine saw and even the Wurlitzer organ.'

Conquest addresses the issue of poetry and 'public taste', but as references to previous critical writings have shown, for many these are topics unavoidably premised on ideas of what is socially and politically healthy. Inevitably Conquest eventually makes the point himself. In the 1940s, he argues, 'it became more plain than is usually the case that without integrity

---

[14]*New Lines*, ed. Robert Conquest, London: Macmillan (1967), pp. xi-xviii. Hereafter *New Lines*.

and judgement enough to prevent surrender to subjective moods or social pressures all the technical and emotional gifts are almost worthless.' While Conquest is not necessarily to be accused of wilful sleight of hand, what he means by surrendering to 'social pressures' is not, I believe, allowing oneself to be side-tracked into writing didactic political poetry, but being influenced by the *wrong* social pressures, thereby producing poetry that fails to conform with his own 'integrity and judgement' in matters social, political and poetic.

New Lines is primarily an attack on the group of 40s poets who called themselves 'Apocalyptics'; but they were by no means wholly representative of the poetry produced in Britain on the eve of, and during the Second World War. It was, however, in Conquest's interests to caricature 40s poetry by way of establishing The Movement as offering a clear alternative, or 'new' poetry. Three Apocalyptic anthologies were produced: *The New Apocalypse* (1939), *The White Horseman* (1941), and *The Crown and the Sickle* (1945). The major contributors included J.F. Hendry, G.S. Fraser, Norman McCaig, Nicholas Moore, Tom Scott and Vernon Watkins. Sympathetic to the group, though never formally a member, was Dylan Thomas. Fraser's Introduction for *The White Horseman* set out the Apocalyptics' manifesto. The movement, he explains:

> embodies what is positive in Surrealism, 'the effort', in Herbert Read's phrase, 'to realize some of the dimensions of man's submerged being'. It denies what is negative – Surrealism's own denial of man's right to exercise conscious control, either of his political and social destinies, or the material offered to him, as an artist, by his subconscious mind. It recognizes, that is, that the intellect and its activity in willed action is part of the living completeness of man, just as the formal element is part of the living completeness of art.[15]

Surrealism, like the Romantic Movement before it, underwent significant modifications in its passage across the English channel. Fraser claimed that the difference between the world of Surrealism and Apocalyptic poetry is 'the difference between the madman, who sits back and contemplates all sorts of trivial relationships, freed from the necessity of action; and a sane man, who accepts dream and fantasy and obscure and terrible desires and energies, as part of his completeness' (*White Horseman* p. 15).

J.F. Hendry's 'Europe: 1939' is an excellent illustration of the Apocalyptic style. At one level the effect of diverse images (dice, bones, geese, shark-teeth), and pending grammatical anarchy, summon up visually surreal effects; yet there remains control, 'the formal element', the sense of a destination for the poem not present, for example, in the verses already quoted by Gascoygne:

---

[15] *The White Horseman*, ed. J.F. Hendry and Henry Treece, London: Routledge (1941), p. 3. Hereafter *White Horseman*.

> Cast in a dice of bones I see the geese of Europe
> Gabble in skeleton jigsaw, and their haltered anger
> Scream a shark-teeth frost through splintering earth and lips
> In the cauldron of Kells I hear man-future fingering
> War and winter barb a world in snow and baptize troops.
>
> (*White Horseman* p. 62)

The Apocalyptics understandably saw themselves at odds with Pound, Eliot, and the New Country poets; they were influenced by the 30s poetry of Gascoygne and George Barker, but looked in particular to D.H. Lawrence as a contemporary source for their theories. Linda Shires has suggested that the adoption of Lawrence was to some extent strategic given the need the group felt for a substantial figure-head. Lawrence's theories of poetic creation were easily interpreted in Apocalyptic terms, and the self-absorption manifest in his posthumous novel *Apocalypse* gave the group an apt title for the late 30s, and a dramatic quotation to follow the title-page of *The White Horseman*.

Among poets of an earlier generation to be admired were Robert Graves and Gerard Manley Hopkins. The tortuous syntax, startling imagery and 'sprung rhythm' of Hopkins's poetry is frequently a feature of Apocalyptic verse. Familiarity with Hopkins was helped by a new edition of his poems brought out in 1930 by Charles Williams.

Graves has been described as 'the first British poet to make full intellectual use of unconscious states of mind' (*Shires* p. 31). Graves, as has recently been pointed out by Peter Kemp, had two potentially contradictory sides to his nature, encapsulated in two of his prose works, *The White Goddess* (1948) and *Goodbye to All That* (1929), 'the fantastic and the factual' (*TLS* 24 Jan. 1986 p. 89). It is easy to see why the Graves who was fascinated by myth, mystery and the occult, and who in 1924 published *The Meaning of Dreams*, should appeal to the Apocalyptics; but his poetry in fact reveals a constant creative tension between the world of the White Goddess and the poet whom Michael Schmidt (a devotee of Movement poetry) chooses to see, a Robert Graves whose 'craftsmanship makes the poems classically impersonal' (*Schmidt* p. 166). Early poems like 'The Pier Glass', 'Down', and subsequently 'In Broken Images' contain what Hendry and his fellow poets were looking for:

> When the fact fails him, he questions his senses;
> When the fact fails me, I approve my senses.
>
> ('In Broken Images' 1938, 11.9–10)

It remains difficult to think of Apocalyptic poetry as the product of a homogeneous group for very long, however. If nothing else, the effect of the war caused most of the group to revise their style. Fraser was one of the first to disclaim his allegiance, turning to a more ordered and less flamboyantly surrealistic style. George Barker had never subscribed, and if we look at his 'Resolution and Dependence' of 1937, it is possible to see why his surrealist imagery attracted the attention of the Apocalyptics, but equally why he did not identify himself with them, and indeed perhaps how he indicates a weakness within the philosophy of the group.

The title, 'Resolution and Dependence' echoes, with a significant modification, the title of one of Wordsworth's best known poems, *Resolution and Independence* (1802), a reflection on the stoical frame of mind of an old leach gatherer, who has faced and come to terms with the uncertainties and difficulties of life in a hostile world. Barker reflects on a society which has failed to learn from the full import of Wordsworth's poetry. Wordsworth, father of the Romantic tradition, has far more to teach us than the contemporary Romantic manifestations of Surrealism.

Barker pictures himself among a crowd outside Bournemouth Pavilion, 'The Palace of Solace'. Among the crowd he recognizes Wordsworth:

> But approaching me with a watch in his hand, he said:
> 'I fear you are fairly early; I expected a man; I see that
> Already your private rebellion has been quelled.
> Where are the violent gestures of the individualist?
> I observe the absence of the erratic, the strange;
> Where is the tulip, the rose, or the bird in the hand?'
> (*Skelton* pp. 186–7)

The parallel between Wordsworth's and Barker's generation is clear. Wordsworth is a poet who has come through a period of 'private rebellion' with something still to say; he still clings, even if it is in a modified form, to his resolution and independence. Contemporary readers choose to know of him only as a superficial nature poet:

> I have passed my hand like a postman's into them;
> The information I dropped in at once dropped out.

Barker is uncomfortably aware that Wordsworth has a good deal more than daffodils to offer the twentieth century. Where 'private rebellion' on its own has proved futile, some alternative must be considered, and in that respect the lake poet is a survivor, despite – as Barker says in the second verse – 'The acute suspicion that Wordsworth is after all dead'. The message this living Wordsworth brings is the resolution to admit the limitations of individualism, of 'the private rebellion, the personal turn', and to recognize that it must lead on to a particular kind of collective responsibility; in other words:

> Not you and not him, not me, but all of them.
> It is the conspiracy of five hundred million
> To keep alive and kick. This is the resolution . . .

The poet who was most obviously an Apocalyptic in style, and yet – despite the adulatory notices he received from the group – remained aloof, was Dylan Thomas (1914–53). Assessment of Thomas's work has always been a matter of controversy. From the first the enthusiasm of Hendry, Treece, Fraser and others was countered by criticism which echoed Geoffrey Grigson's exasperation with 'the Welsh gut-and-gland-and-hair school'.[16] The apparent chaos of imagery and syntax evident in the opening lines of 'In Memory of Ann Jones' (1939) illustrates why Thomas has been accused of self-indulgence, which at worst can seem a cynical manipulation of language for effect rather than meaning:

> After the funeral, mule praises, brays,
> Windshake of sailshaped ears, muffle-toed tap
> Tap happily of one peg in the thick
> Grave's foot, blinds down the lids, the teeth in black,
> The spittled eyes, the salt ponds in the sleeves,
> Morning smack of the spade that wakes up sleep,
> Shakes a desolate boy who slits his throat
> In the dark of the coffin and sheds dry leaves . . .
>   (*Skelton* pp. 122–3)

Apart from the fact that there has always been a readership ready to claim that the effect of such lines is moving, though rationally difficult to explain, it is also the case that Thomas – clearly influenced by Lawrence – offered precise explanations of his theory of how he used images. It is possible to 'explain' the above lines in terms of a concentrated multi-faceted image of the entire event, collapsing the death, the service, the burial and the weather into one experience, a significant part of which for Thomas is the evocation of physical sensation.

The most obvious sign of control in Thomas's work lies in his use of regular line length, and in the rhythmic vitality pointed up by persistent alliteration. The poet's conviction that images forged connections in the mind beyond the realm of immediate, rational discourse, acting both to create and at the same time to challenge meaning is clearly evident in 'And Death Shall Have No Dominion':

> And death shall have no dominion.
> No more may gulls cry at their ears

---

[16]Geoffrey Grigson, *Before the Romantics: An Anthology of the Enlightenment*: Edinburgh: Salamander Press (1984), p. x. First published by Routledge in 1946, the quotation comes from the original Preface. Hereafter *Grigson*.

> Or waves break loud on the seashores;
> Where blew a flower may a flower no more
> Lift its head to the blows of the rain;
> Though they be mad and dead as nails,
> Heads of the characters hammer through daisies;
> Break in the sun till the sun breaks down,
> And death shall have no dominion.
>
> (*Skelton* p. 216–17)

The Romantic connotations of 'blew a flower' are offset by an image of the flower attacked by the wind-blown rain, while the associations implied by 'nails' with death and, more obscurely, with madness, are linked to the fate of flowers brutally and very tangibly being nailed down.

There persists the suspicion for many readers that all this became somehow too easy for Thomas to perform; the inversion of word order in the penultimate line, for example, *'Break* in the *sun* – till the *sun breaks* down' may seem in danger of becoming a too often repeated party trick, trivializing meaning.

The defection of the vast majority of the Auden group from the Marxist poetry of their New Country period, and their subsequent work; Fraser's withdrawal from the Apocalyptics, and indeed the lack of cohesion within the group itself evident from the anthologies; the work of George Barker, David Gascoygne and Dylan Thomas; are all in themselves pointers to the fact that 40s poetry cannot be represented by a cohesive Apocalyptic school. Roy Fuller (b. 1912) was beginning to develop a poetic style in the 1930s which, like that of William Empson, in many respects foreshadows, and was to influence, Movement poetry. Still defined as a 'romantic' by Edward Lucie-Smith when compared with Auden,[17] the basis of Fuller's art lies in his sense of an ordered, rational, often wryly perceived world. 'YMCA Writing Room', written during the war, well illustrates this, with its initial reference to the all-embracing map, 'that coloured square', giving precise, but potentially tragically incomplete information:

> Today my friends were drafted; they are about
> To be exploded, to be scattered over
> That coloured square which in reality
> Is a series of scenes, is boredom, cover,
>
> Nostalgia, labour, death. . . .[18]

The war had a dramatic effect on the style of avant-garde poets like Gascoygne. His Surrealism of the 30s gave way to a bleakness that becomes

---

[17] *British Poetry Since 1945*, ed. Edward Lucie-Smith, Penguin Books (1985) p. 105. Hereafter *Lucie-Smith*.
[18] *Poems of the Second World War*, ed. Victor Selwyn, London: Dent, 'The Oasis Selection' (1985) p. 269. Hereafter *Oasis*.

reminiscent of Imagism in the last four lines of this verse from 'A Wartime Dawn':

> An incommunicable desolation weighs
> Like depths of stagnant water on this break of day. –
> Long meditation without thought. – Until a breeze
> From some pure Nowhere straying, stirs
> A pang of poignant odour from the earth, an unheard sigh
> Pregnant with sap's sweet tang and raw soil's fine
> Aroma, smell of stone, and acrid breath
> Of gravel puddles. While the brooding green
> Of nearby gardens' grass and trees, and quiet flat
> Blue leaves, the distant lilac mirages, are made
> Clear by increasing daylight, and intensified.[19]

If Gascoygne calls to mind Imagist aesthetics, Day Lewis's war-time poetry often recreated a sense of Georgian nostalgia:

> The farmer and I talk for a while of invaders:
> But soon we turn to crops – the annual hope,
> Making of cider, prizes for ewes. Tonight
> How many hearts along this war-mazed valley
> Dream of a day when at peace they may work and watch
> The small sufficient wonders of the countryside.[20]

Despite the fact that in 1939, by way of contrast to 1914, the whole nation found itself potentially on the firing line, the effect on poets was to some extent comparable with 1914–18. The existence of a single, dominating event brought together and tended to remould the variety of styles and schools that had developed between the wars. There is also the fact that the First World War naturally offered itself as a model of how 'war poetry' might be written. One crucial difference was the emergence of a common, widely understood 'cause' to be fought for in 1939. The effect of both world wars in the twentieth century was to create a sense of a temporary but profound disruption if not cessation of the accepted moral and social order within which life was normally conducted.

One response that might reasonably be expected from art in these circumstances, and which arguably became the case with respect to much poetry, was to 'search for structures of beliefs in times of unrelenting chaos' (*Shires* p. 85). Thomas's wartime poetry is generally seen to assume a more formal, controlled nature, and this was evidently true of Gascoygne, Fraser

---

[19] *The Penguin Poets: Contemporary Verse*, ed. Kenneth Allott (1950), p. 247–8.
[20] 'Watching Post', in *Poems of C. Day Lewis 1925–1972*, ed. Ian Parsons, London: Jonathan Cape (1977) p. 137.

and most of the Apocalyptics. The subject of war produced two of Herbert Read's finest poems; from the first war came 'Meditation of a Dying German Officer', written in retrospect (*Silkin* p. 152), and 'A World Within A War' (1940). In both cases Read's normally opaque free verse became toughened and concentrated, revealing an intellectual commitment to his subject normally reserved for his literary criticism.

Nostalgia inevitably becomes attractive and important, keeping memories alive in order to have something in due course to offer the future. Day Lewis has already provided an illustration of this, and in Sidney Keyes's poem 'The Bards' we see how in wartime he believes that the most he can achieve is to preserve the Romantic ideal of the bardic function, rather than practise it:

> Now it is time to remember the winter festivals
> Of the old world, and see their raftered halls
> Hung with hard holly; tongues' confusion; slow
> Beat of the heated blood in those great palaces
> Decked with the pale and sickled mistletoe;
> And voices dying when the blind bard rises . . .[21]

Among poets like Keyes, Alun Lewis and Keith Douglas who saw active service, the latter appears in many respects to be the most obvious throwback to the tradition of First World War poets, particularly with respect to Sassoon. His idealism was countered by his 'near despair over the brutality of war and the waning of aristocratic honour' (*Shires* p. 115), Douglas's poetry seems to spring directly from the experience of a war in which he desperately wanted to take part, and which he was convinced would cost him his life:

> The next month, then, is a window
> and with a crash I'll split the glass.
> Behind it stands one I must kiss,
> person of love or death
> a person or a wraith,
> I fear what I shall find.
>
> (*Oasis* p. 73)

Like Keyes, who was killed in 1943, Douglas was also killed in action in 1944, though ironically in his case death came as the result of an accident rather than from an enemy bullet.

With the onset of a reaction against Modernism which had begun in the late 1920s, the inter-war years were a period when the relationship between

---

[21] Sidney Keyes, *The Collected Poems*, London: Routledge (1945), p. 48.

ideology and poetry became a persistent feature of the way in which poetry was written and critically assessed. The form this debate took can only properly be understood if we recognize not only the impact of Surrealism, but also the way in which contemporaries were looking to the Romantic Movement as a correlative for their situation. If the war had the effect of temporarily stilling that debate, the renewed attack on Romanticism in the 1940s and 50s suggests that there is no reason to suppose it had been terminated. In 1946 Geoffrey Grigson published an anthology of seventeenth and eighteenth-century prose and poetry called *Before the Romantics*. In it he criticized contemporary poetry, insisting that writers should look to the pre-Romantic period of English literature for their models 'if the generality of verse is not to go on liquefying, like a colony of inky-cap toadstools, into a black neo-romantic mixture':

> It is not a reaction I want, not a neo-Georgian bank in red brick among the inky-caps that I would like to build; but, simply, the lean and active verse – and prose – of the Enlightenment, its active and strong habits of mind, do provide us with a control. And we can adapt and apply that control to all we have learned about the inner and curious workings of poetry and ourselves.
>
> (*Grigson* p. x)

The key word is 'control', and later he refers to 'the rules and regulations' which governed the creativity of Pope and Dryden. It is the language of social control as well as artistic control; Grigson recommends the 'Age' with the poetry. Thus a 'neo-mystery mongering Welshman' threatens not just art, but society (*Grigson* p. xi).

If this may be considered a predictable expression of concern after six years of warfare had barely ceased, we should perhaps look also at David Trotter's analysis of ideology and poetry in *The Making of the Reader* (1982). Trotter draws attention to the expressed aims of the periodical, *Poetry Nation*:

> An editorial in the first number of *Poetry Nation* (which later became *PN Review*) announced that the journal would support 'a renewed popularity and practice of clearly formal writing, a common bridling at a vacuous and private rhetoric'. In a supporting essay on 'The Politics of Form', [Michael] Schmidt attacked poets who seek 'to cajole or bemuse the readers'.
>
> When *Poetry Nation* became *PN Review* in 1976, he returned to the theme from a slightly different angle:
>
>> Among modern English writers we have sensed, and gone some way in our early issues towards defining, a failure of seriousness, a flippancy before formal and social choices, and an unwillingness to examine the human implications of certain ideas expressed as it

were casually in particular works of imaginative writing, or in underlying attitudes.

(*Trotter* p. 237)

Setting this against the context of the 1960s, 'when demonstrators who were also unspeakable epic poets ran riot' ('unspeakable epic poets' being another phrase quoted from Schmidt), Trotter concludes that 'the editors of *PN Review* had decided that the level of seriousness demanded by a certain kind of poetry was the same as that demanded by a certain kind of politics':

> 'The critic's task, [Schmidt writes] is to help direct contemporary literature and the modern reader back into the mainstream, reclaiming for both a little of their lost authority. This it may be able to do if there are creative writers worth serious attention, who have refused, with the contraction of the responsive audience and the retreat of the critics, to chasten the scope of their art.'

(*Trotter* p. 238)

The political connotations of 'direct', 'mainstream', 'authority' and 'chasten' are hard to avoid, and whether or not Trotter's conclusions are found to be convincing, his book offers ample evidence for the perpetuation of the literary debate only too openly joined in the inter-war years.

An English Romantic tradition persists through to the present time, and not solely because contemporary critics would seem to be lost without the word. If in no other ways, the Romantic is defined by a continuing belief in the place of the numinous at the centre of the creative act, be it inspired by religion, myth, the occult, the phenomena of the natural world, or an amalgam of them all. One important progenitor of that school was Edith Sitwell, who in the course of time began to realize the ideal of artistic sponteneity through an increasingly powerful mastery of free verse. As the 30s drew to a close, Sitwell's eccentric Bohemian posturing gradually became a progressively angrier and more pointedly satirical stance taken against the hypocrisy of her age. The war, and in particular the manner of its ending, inspired a series of poems which have still to receive the critical attention they merit:

> 'And the fires of your Hell shall not be quenched by the rain
> From those torn and parti-coloured garments of Christ, those
>   rags
> That once were Men. Each wound, each stripe,
> Cries out more loudly than the voice of Cain –
> Saying "Am I my brother's keeper?" ' Think! When the last
>   clamour of the Bought and Sold
> The agony of Gold
> Is hushed. . . . When the last Judas-kiss

Has died upon the cheek of the Starved Man Christ, those ashes
   that were men
Will rise again
to be our Fires upon the Judgement Day!
And yet – who dreamed that Christ has died in vain?
He walks again on the Seas of Blood, He comes in the terrible
   Rain.
>   ('The Shadow of Cain' in *Three Poems of the Atomic Age*,
>   *Sitwell* p. 376)

4
Poetry Since 1945

The effect of the war might reasonably have been expected to be one of clearing the ground for new initiatives and directions in British poetry. Politically, the country certainly appeared to declare itself ready for a break with the past through the Labour Party victory in the General Election of 1945. As the history of that period has been researched and rewritten over the years, Churchill's defeat at the polls is now no longer regarded as an inexplicable aberration, but as a perfectly comprehensible response on the part of the electorate. With the growth in influence and prestige of the BBC during the war, the advent of television, and the continuation of an interventionist role for Government supported by both major political parties after the war, a significantly new situation for the cultural life of the nation swiftly evolved. Initially support for the arts indicated a bid to extend the spirit of a new-found national consensus arising from the country's struggle to defeat Germany. The extent to which such a unity of purpose was real or a product of propaganda has only recently become a subject for serious debate. With the advent of television, however, the spirit of wartime consensus – whatever it actually constituted – began to evaporate.

Krishnan Kumar describes the process as one where 'the collectivist ethos' promoted by 'the great age of radio', imbued with 'the atmosphere of the war and post-war austerity', changed with the coming of television:

> Television announced that the war, and all that went with it, was finally over. Its expansion took place in an era of unprecedented economic growth and rising standards of living. Its associations are with plenty rather than want, leisure rather than work, choice rather than necessity. It belongs to the Macmillan years of consumerism, 'individualism', hedonism, the time when the British people 'never had it so good'. The start of commercial broadcasting in 1954 strongly confirmed these associations. It finally broke the BBC's cultural monopoly, its right and power to speak for and to the nation as a whole, as it had supremely done in wartime. Broadcasting might still aspire to create 'one nation'; it could no longer claim to speak with one voice.[1]

---

[1] *The New Pelican Guide to English Literature* Vol. 8, *The Present*, ed. Boris Ford (1983), pp. 34–5. Hereafter *Pelican Guide VIII*.

One clear tendency for English poets emerging from the experience of the war was to give expression to a sense of relief and deliverance through the celebration of specifically English themes: the countryside, domesticity, in short all the familiar landmarks of English life now no longer under threat of violent eradication. Though not a return to Georgianism in any precise sense, this is poetry rightly seen as belonging to the tradition of which Georgianism was itself only one manifestation. The emphases are inward-looking and reflective, the ideas are rooted in a peculiarly insular, English (rather than British) sense of place. Such poetry is generally seen in America and Europe as still representative of the dominant English tradition which Modernism failed to dislodge early in the century.

In Henry Reed's 'Lessons of the War: 1. Naming of Parts', which swiftly became a favourite anthology piece, it is evident that the lesson to be learnt was precisely that of the beauty of the English countryside at peace:

> This is the lower sling swivel. And this
> Is the upper sling swivel, whose use you will see,
> When you are given your slings. And this is the piling swivel,
> Which in your case you have not got. The branches
> Hold in the gardens their silent, eloquent gestures,
>   Which in our case we have not got.
>
>   (*Oasis* p. 39)

This poem was included by Hermann Peschmann in his comprehensive anthology of British poetry, *The Voice of Poetry 1930-1950* (1950).[2] Peschmann's work with the Workers' Educational Association and London University as an Extension Course Lecturer reflects the post-war conviction that the Government had a duty to democratize educational and cultural opportunities. Noting in his Introduction significant developments in post-war poetry, Peschmann drew attention to 'the emergence of a considerable body of women poets of distinction'. His assessment of their contribution is revealing, pointing towards a revival of Georgian rather than Modernist themes:

> Their verse ranges from the long, musical Virgilian evocations of the English countryside in Vita Sackville-West, or the simple sincerity of Anne Ridler's poetry of family love and domesticity, profoundly permeated with Christian belief and imagery – a poetry with which E.J. Scovell's has obvious affinities – to the deeply felt and exactly observed nature poetry of Ruth Pitter.

Anne Ridler's 'The Phoenix Answered' typifies what Peschmann welcomed; her poetry is primarily concerned with religious experience, but a very English religious experience, here firmly located in an English garden:

---

[2] *The Voice of Poetry 1930-1950*, ed. Hermann Peschmann, London: Evans (1950).

> Sitting in this garden you cannot escape symbols,
>   Take them how you will.
> Here on the lawn like an island where the wind is still,
>   Circled by tides in the field and swirling trees,
>   It is of love I muse,
> Who designs the coloured fronds and heavy umbels,
>   Second-hand marriage, not for passion but business,
>   Brought on by the obliging bees.

If we look at the work of the most popular poet since the war, John Betjeman (1906–84), we find a very similar formula at work. Betjeman's success derives from the fact that he is the poet of what is familiar, recognizable, and dependable:

> Oh the after-tram-ride quiet, when we heard a mile beyond,
> Silver music from the bandstand, barking dogs by Highgate Pond;
> Up the hill where stucco houses in Virginia creeper drown –
> And my childish wave of pity, seeing children carrying down
> Sheaves of drooping dandelions to the courts of Kentish Town.[3]

The apparent ease with which Betjeman created rhythmic patterns, avoiding the crudeness of the nursery-rhyme and hymn book metres they are so clearly based on, and his invocations of a vaguely comforting aura of country parish Anglicanism, are as much a part of his appeal as the whimsical references to familiar place names, car makes and English 'types' which abound in most of the poetry: 'I am a young executive. No cuffs than mine are cleaner;/I have a Slimline brief-case and I use the firm's Cortina.' (*Betjeman* p. 385). Nostalgia is a key ingredient; distaste for the modern, especially if it bears the trademark of an import, is expressed with wit and good humour.

The important thing to understand is that what we are *familiar* with in a Betjeman poem is located essentially in the past; a time when all our poetry rhymed and scanned in much this way; a simpler, innocent past, wistfully remembered. It is nevertheless unwise to take this image of Betjeman's work too much at its face value, despite the fact that he himself was primarily responsible for creating and sustaining it. Avoiding pompous solemnity, and caricaturing a doddery eccentric embalmed in shapeless tweeds arguably gave him and his poetry access to a mass readership otherwise suspicious of art and its pretensions. The other side to this humorous persona, however, expressed itself through a satirical streak the harshness of which, as in 'In Westminster Abbey', could be unmerciful to the very readers he seemed to attract:

---

[3] *John Betjeman's Collected Poems*, Enlarged Edition, London: Murray (1980), pp. 103–4 'Parliament Hill Fields'. Hereafter *Betjeman*.

> Gracious Lord, oh bomb the Germans.
> Spare their women for Thy Sake,
> And if that is not too easy
> We will pardon Thy Mistake.
> But, gracious Lord, whate'er shall be,
> Don't let anyone bomb me.
> <div align="right">(<i>Betjeman</i> p. 91)</div>

In the poems of his later years, nostalgia for the lost landscape, along with the architecture and life-style of pre-war England, was increasingly interrupted by melancholy reflection on his own unhappy childhood, and the fear of death. In 'Aldershot Crematorium' (1974) the natural, felicitous rhythm and rhyme create an effect of helpless inadequacy when coupled with Betjeman's frank admission that even the beauties of biblical phraseology can no longer ward off his doubts:

> But no-one seems to know quite what to say
> (Friends are so altered by the passing years):
> 'Well, anyhow, its not so cold today' –
> And thus we try to dissipate our fears.
> '*I am the Resurrection and the Life*':
> Strong, deep and painful, doubt inserts the knife.
> <div align="right">(<i>Betjeman</i> p. 374)</div>

If Betjeman's ability to create an unprecedentedly broad reading public for his poetry rested on a form of latter-day Georgianism that renders him in many ways unique, the post-war tendency to re-establish an English school of poetry informed by a similarly insular frame of mind was widespread. In the case of The Movement, Robert Conquest's rejection of post-Modernist Romanticism did not inhibit him from using the example set by the first Romantics to assist in redefining a new poetry, untainted by the Modernist and Apocalyptic taste for an essentially alien Surrealism. Conquest not only quoted Aldous Huxley in his Introduction to *New Lines*, he also drew on Coleridge:

> When Coleridge wrote, 'poetry is the blossom and the fragrancy of all human knowledge, human thoughts, human passions, emotions, language', he was expressing the central tradition of all English poetry, classic or romantic.
> <div align="right">(<i>New Lines</i> p. xv)</div>

The particular Romantic trait being emphasized here is that of inclusiveness, and Conquest's implicit criticism of contemporary poetry is that it has been appropriated by a variety of exclusive doctrines, each tending to have its representative style or form. His terminology at the beginning of the Introduction underlines a particular aversion to the influence of Freudian theories of the subconscious:

> In the 1940s the mistake was made of giving the Id, a sound player on the percussion side under a strict conductor, too much of a say in the doings of the orchestra as a whole.
>
> (*New Lines*, p. xi)

Conquest is at pains to emphasize that Movement poetry is the expression of no single doctrine, and consequently there is no one dominant style involved. This is then a very different approach to that initiated by the Imagists, for whom specific issues of style were central to their rejection of Romanticism. Imagist and subsequently Modernist enthusiasm for the use of free verse established a medium understandably attractive to poets influenced by Surrealism, and drawn towards neo-Romanticism in the 1930s and 40s.

Form as an issue in the writing of poetry since the war has naturally remained at the heart of the debate, but the relationship between form and content has not developed along the lines of uncompromising differentiation that the pre-war period indicated might have been the case. Free verse in particular has never won the ground in British poetry that its most committed adherents have sought for it. Geoffrey Thurley characterizes its appeal as 'the dream of absolute spontaneity', arguing – with reference to D.H. Lawrence in particular – that its weakness lies in the way its success 'depends . . . upon the intensity of voice by which it is always governed' (*Thurley* pp. 200–1). Free verse in British poetry remains primarily the province of poets influenced by American Imagists; they form a significant minority including Charles Tomlinson and Basil Bunting, the latter of whom has only relatively recently begun to be recognized as an important voice in British poetry. Among the American poets whose work has been influential in this respect are Ezra Pound, Wallace Stevens, William Carlos Williams and Jack Kerouac; in Bunting's case Louis Zukofsky was also an important mentor.

It is once again to Auden we must turn, 'that large and rational talent' (*New Lines* p. xvii), if we are to appreciate how attitudes to poetic form tended to evolve after the war. In *The Dyer's Hand and Other Essays* (1963) Auden wrote:

> Rhymes, metres, stanza forms, etc., are like servants. If the master is fair enough to win their affection and firm enough to command their respect, the result is an orderly happy household. If he is too tyrannical, they give notice; if he lacks authority, they become slovenly, impertinent, drunk and dishonest . . .
>
> (Quoted in *Thurley* p. 200)

Auden's influence as a 'fair master' of poetic form during and after the war effectively undermined the pre-war tendency to align specific forms with any specific philosophical, aesthetic or socio-political position adopted by the poet. Auden's own position as an ironic observer of the 'eddying muddle' of the human condition after 1939 was clearly established, and he demonstrated how he could make virtually any form dance to his tune at whatever tempo he chose. His personal preferences reflected an increasing respect for Classical models of verse, particularly the epistolary and ode forms used by Horace (65–8 BC). Though this meant that he rarely – if ever – wrote in free verse, the appeal of Horace was undoubtedly the potentially elastic and relaxed structure of a syllabic rather than a metrical framework.[4] In 'Vespers' (1954), from *Horae Canonicae*, he adopted a style best described as heightened prose, a style which reflects the way he read his own poetry.

The poem describes an encounter between Auden himself, 'an Arcadian', and his 'anti-type' (in fact Auden much as he had been in the 30s), 'a Utopian':

> He would like to see me cleaning latrines: I would like to see him removed to some other planet.
>
> Neither speaks. What experience could we possibly share?
>
> Glancing at a lampshade in a store window, I observe it is too hideous for anyone in their senses to buy: He observes it is too expensive for a peasant to buy.
>
> (*Horae Canonicae*, Auden pp. 227–9)

Different as the two men are as types, Auden's final lines are devoted to reflecting on how they are also in fact 'accomplices', the cynical observer of modern life, and the revolutionary committed to class struggle:

> Was it (as it must look to any god of the cross-roads) simply a fortuitous intersection of life-paths, loyal to different fibs,
>
> or also a rendezvous between accomplices who, in spite of themselves, cannot resist meeting
>
> to remind the other (do both, at bottom, desire truth?) of that half of their secret which he would most like to forget,
>
> forcing us both, for a fraction of a second, to remember our victim (but for him I could forget the blood, but for me he could forget the innocence)
>
> on whose immolation (call him Abel, Remus, whom you will, it is one Sin Offering) arcadias, utopias, our dear old bag of a democracy, are alike founded:

---

[4] In syllabic metre the convention of grouping syllables into 'feet' which offer a regular stress pattern (i.e. the iambic foot, a light stress followed by a heavy one), is abandoned in favour of having a fixed number of syllables to a line, allowing the stressed and unstressed accents to vary.

> For without a cement of blood (it must be human, it must be innocent) no secular wall will safely stand.

While no reading of any poem can fail to take account of the part played by its formal presentation, the idea that there are specifically appropriate forms relating to the levels of seriousness and intensity of expression has lost the credence it once had. Milton's creation of an English 'epic' form in the seventeenth century continued to influence poets well on into the nineteenth century, and the idea – if not the form – was at least partially reanimated by Eliot's *Waste Land* in the 1920s. Auden's technical dexterity has been in no small way responsible for the eventual abandonment of the use of form in this manner.

Equally influential in this respect was the revival of interest between the wars in the theoretical statements of the major poets of the Romantic Movement. Wordsworth in particular had been prepared to defy the association of profound thought with its traditional poetic forms in *Lyrical Ballads*. The spirit of the Preface to *Lyrical Ballads* could be invoked against those who argued that the possibilities of traditional nineteenth-century verse forms had been exhausted. Auden's poetry after 1939 appears in retrospect to have created the dominant and pervasive tone for poetry of the immediate postwar period, and then to have gone on to have a lasting effect. Debunking the grand manner with lines like 'loyal to different fibs', and 'our dear old bag of a democracy' carried with it a clear message. The role of the poet was to be redefined; the apocalyptic and visionary possibilities were rejected in favour of a more prosaic observation of humanity coping with life as it is. The Shelley identified by Read, 'in conflict with the social imposition of normality', and expressing 'an organic urge towards "a completer oneness of life" ' which ultimately threatens apocalyptic social and political change, gives way to something akin to what Read refers to as 'the dry air of disillusion' (*Shelley* pp. 177–8, 197).

Philip Larkin's account of his search for a mentor is representative; initially it was to Yeats, the latter-day Romantic that he turned; but Yeats was superseded by Thomas Hardy, whose fatalistic rejection of Romantic optimism informs all of Larkin's mature work:

> What are days for?
> Days are where we live.
> They come, they wake us
> Time and time over.
> They are to be happy in:
> Where can we live but days?
>
> Ah, solving that question
> Brings the priest and the doctor
> In their long coats
> Running over the fields.[5]

---

[5]'Days', in *The Whitsun Weddings*, London: Faber & Faber (1964), p. 27. Hereafter *Whitsun Weddings*.

'Days are where we live', the question is answered. If we are tempted to make a question of the answer, the consequence, described with a humorously surrealist sketch of the priest and the doctor, can be madness. Do you want such a visitation? Given Larkin's picture of them in their long coats, the answer is assumed to be no. The moral of the poem is contained partly in his ironic decision to adopt that most dangerously subjective poetic form free verse.

Larkin established himself as a poet whose influence and reputation were based on his individual achievement, rather than as the representative of any particular 'school'. The consensus is now that he was a great poet, though there remain those who strongly argue a contrary view. (See Michael Kirkham, 'Philip Larkin and Charles Tomlinson: Realism and Art', in *Pelican Guide* VIII.) He certainly fulfilled the Movement's desire to belittle the apocalyptic role of poetry rooted in the neo-Romantic tradition. Repeatedly, Larkin's verdict on the poet who seeks to break out of this reality to find a more spiritually noble reality is that it is dishonest, if not criminally misleading. In 'Poetry of Departures' he admits that his own dissatisfaction with the world in which he is constrained to live tempts him to make a fittingly Byronic gesture:

> Yes, swagger the nut-strewn roads,
> Crouch in the fo'c'sle
> Stubbly with goodness, if
> It weren't so artificial,
> Such a deliberate step backwards
> To create an object:
> Books; china; a life
> Reprehensibly perfect.[6]

Rhyme and syllabic regularity from verse to verse supply the underlying maintenance of control in this poem (with the appropriate exception of line 5 in this final verse), and the effect is to whip us back into line, as he does in 'Toads':

> Ah, were I courageous enough
> To shout *Stuff your pension*!
> But I know, all too well, that's the stuff
> That dreams are made on . . .
>   (*Less Deceived* pp. 32–3)

---

[6] *The Less Deceived*, Irthlingborough: Marvell Press (1977), p. 34. First published in 1955. Hereafter *Less Deceived*.

'Poetry of Departures' has an interesting nineteenth-century point of reference in Robert Browning's 'Waring', a poem written in the 1840s which stands by the Romantic dream of opting out of society that Larkin evidently finds so distasteful:

> What's become of Waring
> Since he gave us all the slip,
> Chose land-travel or sea-faring,
> Boots and chest or staff and scrip,
> Rather than pace up and down
> Any longer London town?

Quoting Larkin simply to reveal evidence of Movement attitudes is to be unfair to his best work. In longer poems such as 'Church Going' and 'The Whitsun Weddings' he does far more than simply come lugubriously to terms with the boredom of life's 'threadbare perspectives' ('Triple Time', *Less Deceived* p. 35). The formal solemnity of 'Church Going' is of a genuinely profound nature, the irony sufficiently restrained to avoid what in other poems can degenerate into mere spite. The church, a symbol of spirituality, of a life which transcends the immediate tawdry world, does impose an 'awkward reverence' on the poet; and if the main themes are the building's imminent redundancy, and religious faith seen as a comforting falsehood, the final verses do in fact claw back a glimmer of hope. Half way through the poem we read:

> But superstition, like belief, must die,
> And what remains when disbelief has gone?
> Grass, weedy pavement, brambles, buttress, sky,
>
> A shape less recognizable each week,
> A purpose more obscure. . . .

In the final verse, however, Larkin's predeliction for despair is countered by an unironic appeal to seriousness:

> A serious house on serious earth it is,
> In whose blent air all our compulsions meet,
> Are recognized, and robed as destinies.
> And that much never can be obsolete,
> Since someone will forever be surprising
> A hunger in himself to be more serious,
> And gravitating with it to this ground,
> Which, he once heard, was proper to grow wise in,
> If only that so many dead lie round.
> (*Less Deceived* pp. 28–9)

'The Whitsun Weddings' is remarkable in the first instance for its powerful rhythmic and visual evocation of the train journey it describes:

> All afternoon, through the tall heat that slept
>   For miles inland,
> A slow and stopping curve southwards we kept.
> Wide farms went by, short-shadowed cattle, and
> Canals with floatings of industrial froth;
> A hothouse flashed uniquely: hedges dipped
> And rose: and now and then a smell of grass
> Displaced the reek of buttoned carriage-cloth
> Until the next town, new and nondescript,
> Approached with acres of dismantled cars.

The final line is an excellent example of Larkin's unfailing gift of knowing when, over against precise description, to exaggerate to good effect. His treatment of the wedding parties gathered at each station to see off the newlyweds is typically abrasive. The idea that here are people attempting some form of ritualized escape from reality, and managing only to be coarse, ridiculous or pathetic is conveyed with impressive economy:

> The fathers with broad belts under their suits
> And seamy foreheads; mothers loud and fat;
> An uncle shouting smut; and then the perms,
> The nylon gloves and jewellery-substitutes,
> The lemons, mauves, and olive-ochres that
>
> Marked off the girls unreally from the rest.

Yet despite the cynicism, there is also a tenderness and compassion towards the young couples which derives, perhaps, from the fact that he finds himself able to identify with them through the shared experience of the journey. The final verse, linking the arrival of the train and its passengers with an image of rain in the dry and arid landscape of 'London spread out in the sun', is left to counter the patent unreality of the way we choose to celebrate the beginning of married life (*Whitsun Weddings* pp. 21–3).

Larkin was a gifted observer of the details of daily life, and the popularity of his poetry relates to its unpretentious precision, and the impression we get of an 'ordinary' person behind it. Though Betjeman played up to the role of an ingenuous eccentric over against Larkin's hermit-crab existence at Hull, it is not difficult to see how in many ways their work is complementary. Betjeman had a high regard for Larkin's poetry, and Larkin's appreciation of Betjeman is to be gauged by the fact that he was prepared to let Betjeman lead him through the awkward silences of a BBC television portrait of himself, working and writing in Hull. Being identified with a school of poetry, and even more, as a major voice within it, was repellent to him. Inclusion in The Movement proved to be an unexpected embarrassement for a number of poets included in *New Lines*. Elizabeth Jennings made it clear that her association with The Movement was likely to create a positive barrier for those wishing to understand her work (see *Lucie-Smith* p. 129).

Conquest's reasons for including her are not difficult to appreciate. Her poetry continually calls attention to the barriers she senses standing between objective reality, 'the certain, solid thing', and the spiritual life ('Song At The Beginning Of Autumn', *New Lines* p. 4). Jennings's misgivings about Movement poetry were that it embodied an attack on the centrality of the spiritual life, and despite her constant reference to a clear and often frustrating divide between a physical existence and a numinous world identified with nature, where the physical seems always to have the upper hand, it is the importance of the numinous she wishes to stress:

> Do I control what I can contemplate
> Or is it my vision that's amenable?
> I turn in my mind, my mind is a room whose wall
> I can see the top of but never completely scale.
> ('In The Night', *New Lines* pp. 7–8)

Windows and walls are frequently used by Jennings to symbolize the barrier between a richly spiritual and an inhibitingly physical existence, but in this poem it is ultimately the rationalizing process of 'thought' over against emotion which binds the poet to a world of physical reality.

Where Jennings sees this situation in terms of a dynamic tension, Conquest was presumably reading her in a more pessimistic light. Her formal use of rhyme and metre were certainly in accord with Movement principles, but again, poet and critic have interpreted the effect differently. In more recent work Elizabeth Jennings has experimented with free verse and prose poetry. From the outset, however, as Edward Lucie-Smith has suggested, she was 'a more romantic, outgoing writer than those she was grouped with' (*Lucie-Smith* p. 129). Lucie-Smith's use of the term 'romantic' to differentiate Jennings from other Movement poets is important. Nowhere is the nature of the contrast more striking than with D.J. Enright's contribution to *New Lines*. In 'The Interpreters' he writes:

> One thinks of those critics for whom the outside is a dreadful bore:
> they scrape for the ambiguous, dig for the profound, deep, deep
>   beneath the ground –
> what you read on the surface of the agitated page is only an idle
>   dusty weed.
> (*New Lines* pp. 60–2)

In a prosaic form reminiscent of Auden's 'Vespers', 'The Interpreters' attacks in the first instance critics bent on mystifying art, rather than poets. The poets referred to, however, are those committed to unambiguous meaning, those who 'sing of the merely real'. From its inception, Romanticism had challenged the 'merely real'. What belongs on the far side of the wall in 'In The Night' is the very thing Enright distrusts, be it 'a glittering fragment of/Zen', or a 'mysterious metaphysical temptation' ('The Interpreters' v. 5). Limited as the settings of Jenning's poems often are, their underlying themes remain identifiable as expressions of a central tenet of Romanticism. She continually questions the extent to which experience may be defined in empirical, physical and material terms. Introversion causes the boundaries of reality to become increasingly indistinct in opposition to the limits imposed by the rational mind.

The choice of Thom Gunn (b. 1929) for *New Lines* was less problematical. In 1956 he was still a poet known for his strict adherence to formal style. This was to change following his decision to settle in the United States, and the account of Gunn most frequently given now is of a poet losing his sense of direction and purpose. Michael Schmidt evidently regrets the loss of formality in his work:

> Surrendering time perspective and prescriptive form, he is in danger of giving us raw moments which are not poems, which are merely notes, irrelevant because not intense in the way they are communicated.
>
> (*Schmidt* p. 382)

The recurring theme of Gunn's poetry is nihilism; the shedding of peripheral details in search of the self, 'Knowing possession means the risk of loss'. 'Merlin In The Cave: He Speculates Without A Book' was therefore a fitting poem for *New Lines*. Merlin, the great magician, has been stripped of his powers and walled up in a cave. Only he himself is left to give meaning to his existence, 'But I must act, and make/The meaning in each movement that I take' (*New Lines* pp. 34–7). The effort is essentially that which Larkin has to make, where repeatedly he depicts himself debarred from the fictions and illusions used by others to live their lives, whether they be wedding parties or church congregations. Never far beneath the surface for both poets, consequently, is the prospect that 'Beneath it all, desire of oblivion runs' (Larkin, 'Wants', *Less Deceived* p. 22).

Gunn never shared Larkin's morose diffidence, but in 'Modes of Pleasure', essentially the same conclusion is reached. Writing there of 'The Fallen Rake' he explains:

> The very beauty of his prime
> Was that the triumphs which recurred
> In different rooms without a word
> Would all be lost some time in time.[7]

---

[7] *The New Poetry*, ed. A. Alvarez, Penguin Books (1966), pp. 164–5. Hereafter *New Poetry*.

In America, Gunn's nihilism led him to identify increasingly with the sense of rootlessness prevalent in the youth cult of the time, and in consequence he himself became something of a cult poet of the drop-out syndrome. More self-consciously intellectual and exhibitionist than Larkin, the quality of pent-up violence in his poetry remained for the most part an attack on the Romanticism which informed Elizabeth Jenning's work. In 'On The Move', the motorcyclists are portrayed romantically, but it is a romance engendered wholly by them; if they have a 'meaning', it is 'in *their* noise':

> On motorcycles, up the road, they come:
> Small, black, as flies hanging in heat, the Boys,
> Until the distance throws them forth, their hum
> Bugles to thunder held by calf and thigh
> In goggles, donned impersonality,
> In gleaming jackets trophied with the dust,
> They strap in doubt – by hiding it, robust –
> And almost hear a meaning in their noise.
> (*New Poetry* pp. 156–7)

Like Gunn, Donald Davie's style has altered considerably since Conquest published him in *New Lines*. Davie remains, however, an Augustan in spirit, believing in 'a reassertion of the validity of syntactical clarity, traditional forms, and reason' (*Schmidt* p. 321). It is important to remember that the poet who in the late 1950s seemed to represent the spirit of Conquest's *New Lines* Introduction most precisely, identified himself wholeheartedly with the Augustan tradition of satire; note in the following extract from 'Too Late For Satire' not only the imitation of Pope's style, but the by now statutory jibe at the 'Id' of Freudian modernity:

> I might have been as pitiless as Pope
> But to no purpose . . .
> To blame is lame, and satirists are late.
> No knife can stick in history or the id,
> No cutlass carve us from the lime of fate.
> (*New Lines* pp. 68–9)

In 1962 Penguin Books published *The New Poetry*, an anthology selected and introduced by A. Alvarez. The selection was a personal one, in itself not intended to identify a particular school of poets. Alvarez's Introduction, however, 'The New Poetry or Beyond The Gentility Principle', registered a clear protest aimed primarily at the *New Lines* anthology. Poetry, Alvarez wrote, 'needs . . . a new seriousness'; the prevailing fashion, headed by The Movement, was for 'gentility':

> . . . a belief that life is always more or less orderly, people always more or less polite, their emotions and habits more or less decent and

more or less controllable; that God, in short, is more or less good.

(*New Poetry* p. 25)

Poets should tackle head-on the major issues of their time; and in attempting to define those issues, Alvarez insists that they exist conceptually as well as in terms of their tangible manifestations:

> What, I suggest, has happened in the last half century is that we are gradually being made to realize that all our lives, even those of the most genteel and enislanded, are influenced profoundly by forces which have nothing to do with gentility, decency or politeness. Theologians would call these forces evil, psychologists, perhaps, libido. Either way, they are forces of disintegration which destroy the old standards of civilization. Their public faces are those of two world wars, of the concentration camps, and the threat of nuclear war.
>
> (*New Poetry* p. 26)

The ironic dismissal by Movement poets of the language of psychologists and priests won't do; 'gentility' is no defence, the poet must attempt to confront the forces at work within modern society 'nakedly and without evasion' (*New Poetry* p. 29).

Alvarez insisted that he was not laying down what poets should write about, nor how they should do it; his discussion centres in the end on a plea for a full engagement with both 'experience' and 'intelligence'. This is effectively an argument which claims the Romantic tradition still has a role to play in the writing of post-war poetry; the attempt to suppress or ignore emotion in favour of 'intelligence' (a post-Freudian over-reaction) can no longer be justified. The Movement has its strengths, not least a recognition of poetic discipline, 'which is vital if the art is to remain public' (*New Poetry* p. 29). But essentially the thrust of the argument is for the reinstatement of the numinous in the act of poetic creation, and a broadening of perspectives to learn from American poetry. Ted Hughes's poem, 'A Dream Of Horses', is preferred to Larkin's 'At Grass' because Hughes is attempting to impart to the reader 'a powerful complex of emotions and sensations'; the horses about which Hughes writes 'reach back, as in a dream, into a nexus of fear and sensation. Their brute world is part physical, part state of mind' (*New Poetry* p. 31).

Hughes's poetry certainly does stand in marked contrast to anything included in *New Lines*. Charles Tomlinson diagnoses *New Lines* as revealing a 'deliberate narrowing' in British poetry. For Tomlinson, Movement poetry may be summed up as 'an excuse . . . for the British philistine', and he quotes by way of illustration Larkin's statement that he had 'no belief in "tradition" or a common myth-kitty or casual allusions in poems to other poems or poets' (*Pelican Guide VIII* pp. 450–1). In practice, as we have seen in 'Poetry of Departures', this independence from the past was virtually impossible to sustain.

The centrality of myth for Hughes, his interest in the occult, in the idea of the poet as shaman – one who can enter the spirit world through trance – and his recognition of a poetic tradition from Anglo-Saxon poetry through to Wilfred Owen, Hopkins, D.H. Lawrence and Dylan Thomas, has given rise to a succession of poems that fulfil, in Martin Dodsworth's view, the demands of post-war Romanticism:

> ... a Romantic poetry ... that prefers individual insight to the conventional values of its society, and that tends to see itself as a privileged, indeed sovereign and unique, way of looking at life and judging it.
> *(Pelican Guide VIII* p. 281)

What Hughes seeks is of an elemental nature; he is the last poet of this postwar period we might expect to find impressed by the 'Gentility Principle', and his reputation as an animal poet arises from his use of animals to investigate the world human beings inhabit beyond their assumed gentility. 'The Horses' from his first collection of poems, *The Hawk In The Rain* (1957), powerfully evokes a transcendental experience triggered off by the sunrise:

> Slowly detail leafed from the darkness. Then the sun
> Orange, red, red erupted.
>
> Silently, and splitting to its core tore and flung cloud,
> Shook the gulf open, showed blue ...[8]

The fragmentary form, the evident debt to Hopkins and Anglo-Saxon alliterative verse ('splitting to its core tore and flung cloud'), and the violent twisting of language towards incoherence, are all evidence of an individual attempting with uncertain success to penetrate the elemental forces of life. On his way to the moor ridge, the poet encounters the horses, standing 'Megalith-still' in the half-darkness before dawn. Returning, he sees them once more in the dawn light. They are naturally, effortlessly, a part of the mystery, the mystery referred to by Isaac Rosenberg in 'Break Of Day In The Trenches' as 'the same old druid Time as ever'. Only man, it seems, is left to stumble forward in alienation; Hughes depicts himself as agitated to the point of delirium by the experience of the sunrise.

The poem ends with an unmistakable echo of Wordsworth's famous 'Daffodil' poem of 1804. Having taken strength from the sight of the flowers by the lakeside, Wordsworth had concluded:

> For oft, when on my couch I lie
> In vacant or in pensive mood,
> They flash upon that inward eye
> Which is the bliss of solitude;
> And then my heart with pleasure fills,
> And dances with the daffodils.

[8] Ted Hughes, *Selected Poems 1957–81*, London: Faber & Faber (1982) p. 19. Hereafter *Hughes*.

Hughes concludes his poem with the following lines:

> In din of crowded streets, going among the years, the faces,
> May I still meet my memory in so lonely a place
>
> Between the streams and the red clouds, hearing curlews,
> Hearing the horizons endure.
>
> *(Hughes* p. 20)

It would be truer to say that Hughes's lines combine the visionary element of the experience signified in 'I wandered lonely as a cloud' with the fear expressed by Wordsworth in *Resolution and Independence*; the landscape of 'The Horses' belongs to the latter poem, as does Hughes's phrase 'in so lonely a place'.

Hughes, Michael Schmidt suggests, writes out of a sense of the 'dislocations' of his time, cultural, historical and psychological; his poetry reveals 'a sense of the inadequacy of humanism, the bankruptcy of the old symbols, and a gradual recognition of the bankruptcy of the old forms' (*Schmidt* p. 384). Common ground with the Romantic Movement is therefore not difficult to understand, nor is the fact that Hughes consciously seems to place 'The Horses' within that tradition. The poet's role is one of positive exploration and invention; and creative energy – often finding expression through images of violence – is always evident in Hughes's work. As a post-war Romantic, however, the emphasis has been on disintegration and the loss of wholeness in 'the split personality of modern man', in marked contrast to the Wordsworthian and Coleridgean ideal of an organically unified existence.[9]

The central theme of both *Wodwo* (1967) and *Crow* (1970) is the search through a nightmare world for an illusive completeness. Crow is a mythic creation who eternally questions the orthodox view of the world by being something less than human, the consequence of which is that he outrageously threatens to become something more. Thus in 'A Horrible Religious Error', while God watches humanity bowing down in fear before evil in its newly created serpent form with a grimace that could imply either sheer malevolence, or an inability to control what he has made:

> ... Crow only peered.
>   Then took a step or two forward,
>   Grabbed this creature by the slackskin nape,
>   Beat the hell out of it, and ate it.
>
> *(Hughes* p. 121)

Hughes (b. 1930), like Larkin, has established a poetic voice recognized primarily as his own, rather than as representing any particular school.

---

[9]Hughes quoted in the 1970 edition of *Lucie-Smith* p. 390. Hereafter *Lucie-Smith 1970*.

Having said that, however, his poetry has had a profound influence on postwar poetry reacting against Movement tendencies. The so-called Group, a set of poets who began meeting in the mid-1950s, were equally concerned to challenge Movement aesthetics with inventive, and often angry poetry which aligned them to some extent with the work of Wesker and Osborne in the theatre. Group poets included Philip Hobsbaum, its founder member, Peter Porter, Peter Redgrove, Edward Lucie-Smith and George MacBeth. In MacBeth's poem 'Owl', the influence of Hughes is clear. The emphasis is on the violence of the bird, 'Torn meat/from the sky. Owl lives/by the claws of his brain' (*Lucie-Smith* pp. 186-7. Compare 'Hawk Roosting', *Hughes* p. 43).

The celebration of brute strength and aggression for which many of Hughes's animal poems are noted signifies an impatience not just with the conformist – even hang-dog – tone of Movement poetry; it implies a rejection of the whole ethos of post-war 'consensus' politics. Political issues in Hughes remain a matter of general statement, identified in the context of a world part mythic, part 'natural'. But if Hughes's response to contemporary English society, what he called 'this tame corner of civilization' (*Lucie-Smith 1970* p. 390), emerges as reactionary, it by no means follows that other poets influenced by him reflected his views.

Seamus Heaney (b. 1939), the first of a group of Northern Irish poets to become an important new influence in the late 1960s and 1970s, was drawn to Hughes for his 'combination of ritual intensity, prose readiness, direct feeling and casual speech . . . fetching energy and ancestry from what is beyond the Pale and beneath the surface'. Hughes's poetry, Heaney writes, 'recalled English poetry in the 1950s from a too suburban aversion of the attention from the elemental; and the poems beat the bounds of a hidden England in streams and trees, on moors and byres'.[10] Heaney's concern for tradition and for what Larkin had dismissed as 'myth-kitties', stems in part from his sense of himself as an Irish poet influenced deeply by English literature. As it had been for Yeats, the relationship with England and the English and their culture is fraught with contradictions. The English Romantic poets, Keats, Blake and specifically Wordsworth, are important to him in particular ways:

> [Wordsworth's] great strength and originality as a writer came first of all from his trusting the validity of his experience, from his courageous and visionary determination to *érige en lois ses impressions personnels*. But the paraphrasable content of Wordsworth's philosophy of nature would remain inert had he not discovered the sounds proper to his sense.
>
> (*The Makings of a Music*, in *Preoccupations* p. 69)

---

[10] *Englands of the Mind* (1976), in Seamus Heaney, *Preoccupations: Selected Prose 1968-1978*, London: Faber & Faber (1980), p. 157, 153. Hereafter *Preoccupations*.

'Sounds proper to . . . sense' is a phrase expressing a central poetic tenet for Heaney. His own sensitivity to the properties of individual words, of rhythm and the nuances of rhyme, has led him to a high regard for Gerard Manley Hopkins. It is important to appreciate what it is he argues Hopkins achieves in his language, as against, for example, Keats: 'In Keats, the rhythm is narcotic, in Hopkins it is a stimulant to the mind. Keats woos us to receive, Hopkins alerts us to perceive' (*The Fire I' The Flint*, in *Preoccupations* p. 85). It is the active, creative principle identified in Hughes that is found also in Hopkins.

The most immediate influence on Heaney as a young poet was Philip Hobsbaum, and Heaney's description of Hobsbaum's impact on the poetry scene in Belfast in the mid 1960s is important:

> He was impatient, dogmatic, relentlessly literary: yet he was patient with those he trusted, unpredictably susceptible to a wide variety of poems and personalities and urgent that the social and political exacerbations of our place should disrupt the decorums of literature.
> (*Belfast*, in *Preoccupations* p. 29)

The ground was prepared for the summer of 1969 when sectarian violence in Northern Ireland flared up with renewed intensity. 'From that moment,' writes Heaney, 'the problems of poetry moved from being simply a matter of achieving the satisfactory verbal icon to being a search for images and symbols adequate to our predicament' (*Feeling Into Words*, in *Preoccupations* p. 56).

Heaney's early work had been essentially autobiographical, though a wider historical context is generally evident. It surfaces, for example, in 'At A Potato Digging' from his first collection, *Death of a Naturalist* (1966):

> Like crows attacking crow-black fields, they stretch
> A higgledy line from hedge to headland;
> Some pairs keep breaking ragged ranks to fetch
> A full creel to the pit and straighten, stand
>
> Tall for a moment but soon stumble back
> To fish new load from the crumbled surf.
> Heads bow, trunks bend, hands fumble towards the black
> Mother. Processional stooping through turf
>
> Recurs mindlessly as autumn. Centuries
> Of fear and homage to the famine god
> Toughen the muscles behind their humbled knees,
> Make a seasonal altar of the sod.[11]

Death of a Naturalist indicates Heaney's attachment to formal verse patterns, but his preparedness to experiment is also evident. The rhythmic

---

[11]In *Selected Poems 1965-1975*, London: Faber & Faber (1980), pp. 21-3. Hereafter *Heaney S.P.*

movement of these lines is subtly varied as is the use of half-rhyme within lines. The full effect of

$$\text{Ă hígg-lĕ-dў línė}$$

is realized by the imperfect match of 'hedge' and 'head(land)'; '... from hedge to headland' enacts the uneven line of labourers, constantly breaking and reforming, an image also reinforced by conflating land and sea, 'To fish a new load from the crumbled surf.' Heaney's use of imagery often achieves its impact through an Imagistic merging process; the soil is not merely like surf, the images blend to create a medium freshly perceived, with new meanings implicit: 'the black/Mother'.

The general effect of these verses is representative of the volume as a whole; a reasonably formal, leisurely, contemplative style, but often startling for what Anthony Thwaite has described as Heaney's 'verbal and physical precision'.[12] The return of a particularly violent phase in the political situation of Ireland did not result in a new departure into politicized 'public' poetry for Heaney. The 'predicament' of the 1970s, 'the religious intensity of the violence' and 'its deplorable authenticity' was of necessity a part of the experience from which poetry would come; but Heaney sees the function of poetry as essentially an act of reconciliation operating at a psychological level. The Irish Catholic and Ulster Protestant cling to 'bankrupt psychology and mythologies'; poetry redefines the issue in terms of 'befitting emblems of adversity' (*Feeling Into Words*, *Preoccupations* pp. 56–8). Initially Heaney found the 'emblem' he sought in P.V. Glob's account of Iron Age society based on the evidence of preserved bodies of men and women discovered in the bogs of Jutland. Many were sacrificial victims, and the notion of a continuing ritual process of sacrifice to an earth Goddess ('the black/Mother') suggested parallels that set Ireland in the 1970s in a new perspective:

> ... this is more than an archaic barbarous rite: it is an archetypal pattern. And the unforgettable photographs of these victims blended in my mind with photographs of atrocities, past and present, in the long rites of Irish political and religious struggles.
>
> <div align="right">(<i>Preoccupations</i> pp. 57–8)</div>

Heaney suggests that the contemporary diagnosis of Ireland's problems is misguided, and reveals a cultural dislocation that has had tragic consequences. In this respect he echoes what Yeats believed, but where Yeats turned for an antidote to the power of folk-memory transmitted through symbolism, Heaney's intention has been to redefine the root causes of the country's violent recent history within the context of primeval forces:

---

[12] Anthony Thwaite, *Poetry Today: A Critical Guide to British Poetry 1960–1984*, London: Longman (1985), p. 110.

> Out there in Jutland
> In the old man-killing parishes
> I will feel lost,
> Unhappy and at home.
> ('The Tollund Man', *Heaney S.P.* p. 79)

Compared with *Death of a Naturalist*, the poetry of the later volumes becomes more sparse, at times little more than a series of terse descriptions building one upon the other as the peat bogs, depositories of the past, have done. We are reminded of Hughes at his most minimal, perhaps, but the poetry is in no way derivative:

> Ruminant ground,
> digestion of mollusc
> and seed pod,
> deep pollen bin.
>
> Earth-pantry, bone-vault,
> sun-bank, embalmer
> of votive goods
> and sabred fugitives.
> Insatiable bride.
> Sword-swallower,
> casket, midden,
> floe of history.
> ('Kinship', *Heaney S.P.* p. 120)

In the final section of 'Kinship' (from *North*, 1975), he suggests that if the Roman historian Tacitus were to return now, he would find very little changed:

> Come back to this
> 'island of ocean'
> where nothing will suffice.
> Read the inhumed faces
>
> of casualty and victim;
> report us fairly,
> how we slaughter
> for the common good
>
> and shave the heads
> of the notorious,
> how the goddess swallows
> our love and terror.
> (*Heaney S.P.* p. 124)

Heaney's preoccupation with the bog people dominated *A Northern Hoard* and *North*; direct reference to 'the troubles' and to his own sense of inadequacy as a poet having to confront the issue occurs in several of the poems in *Field Work* (1979). In 'Casualty' he describes a drinking friend killed by a terrorist bomb:

> But my tentative art
> His turned back watches too:
> He was blown to bits
> Out drinking in a curfew
> Others obeyed, three nights
> After they shot dead
> The thirteen men in Derry.
> PARAS THIRTEEN, the walls said,
> BOGSIDE NIL. That Wednesday
> Everybody held
> His breath and trembled.[13]

The uneven lines falter, rhyme and half-rhyme hold the structure together, and the idiom moves between the consciously poetic, 'my tentative art', and the partisan slogans.

The dead man is described as one who made the poet question the point of his work, the more so because Heaney feels a genuine respect for him:

> I loved his whole manner,
> Sure-footed but too sly,
> His deadpan sidling tact,
> His fisherman's quick eye
> And turned observant back.

A resolution is effected by a skilful conflation of the different worlds the two men inhabit. Rhyme and rhythm and imagery in these lines are superbly crafted to endorse the idea that the fisherman's task and that of the poet are intimately related:

> I tasted freedom with him.
> To get out early, haul
> Steadily off the bottom,
> Dispraise the catch, and smile
> As you find a rhythm
> Working you, slow mile by mile,
> Into your proper haunt
> Somewhere, well out, beyond . . .

---

[13] *Field Work*, London: Faber & Faber (1979) pp. 21–4. Hereafter *Fieldwork*.

> Dawn-sniffing revenant,
> Plodder through midnight rain,
> Question me again.

Other poets in Heaney's position have been more direct, both in their depiction of contemporary Ireland and in their concern at what the poet's role might be. Derek Mahon's irregular line length and line setting comes close to creating visually the scarcely suppressed hysteria of 'Rage for Order':

> Somewhere beyond the scorched gable end and the burnt-out
>   buses
>   there is a poet indulging
>   his wretched rage for order –
> or not as the case may be; for his
>   is a dying art,
> an eddy of semantic scruples . . .
>
> *(Lucie-Smith* p. 351)

Tom Paulin writes with a constant sense of formal control and 'tradition' informing his work, he lacks Heaney's lyricism, but the syntactical and rhythmic complexities of, for example, 'Under the Eyes' are a crucial part of the poem's expression:

> The city is built on mud and wrath.
> Its weather is predicted; its streetlamps
> Light up in the glowering, crowded evenings.
> Time-switches, ripped from them, are clamped
> To sticks of sweet, sweating explosive . . .[14]

Paul Muldoon's poetry has a less academically worked quality than that of Paulin, relying far more on a polished satirical wit reminiscent at times of Auden. In 'Anseo', he describes how a child whom no one took seriously at school ended up as an IRA Commandant. As children they would all respond with the Irish word 'Anseo' to the schoolmaster as he called the roll, the unfortunately named Joseph Mary Plunkett Ward invariably being the butt of the master's sarcastic jokes:

> And he told me, Joe Ward,
> Of how he had risen through the ranks
> To Quartermaster, Commandant:
> How every morning at parade
> His volunteers would call back *Anseo*

---

[14] *The Penguin Book of Contemporary British Poetry*, ed. Blake Morrison and Andrew Motion (1982) p. 116. Hereafter *CBP*.

> And raise their hands
> As their names occurred.
>
> (*Lucie-Smith* pp. 360–1)

In every respect, despite in a number of cases a debt to Movement poetry (Larkin in particular), Irish poetry of the 1960s and 70s continued, as Hughes had done, to challenge the post-war insularity of English poetry. The late 1950s and 60s had already opened up possibilities for new directions in poetry quite apart from the tenor of work by Hughes, Alvarez and the poets of Hobsbaum's original Group. 1960s Pop culture, the fruit of the so-called 'permissive society' in which the young sought cultural and moral independence from their elders, bred a particular style of iconoclasm in art. Most significantly it established through the music industry a poetry-with-music idiom. During a relatively brief period of affluence the 'angry young men' and Aldermarston marchers of the late 50s joined with the various youth cults of the 60s to create the mystique of the 'swinging sixties' in London and the provinces (Liverpool in particular), a movement of sufficient strength even to stem the tide of Americanization in popular music, films, television and fashion.

With the creation of the post-war pop music industry, a new medium was available for an 'alternative' poetry. At its most interesting barriers could be erased between 'serious' modern music, progressive jazz, folk and pop; musicologists with reputations in the field of high culture like Wilfred Mellors were moved to turn their attention to Beatles music and lyrics. Among the products of a cynically commercial music world, lyrics protesting at the hypocrisy of contemporary moral and political standards began to find a place. The words were often in themselves simplistic expressions of anger or outrage, relying to a considerable degree on the rhythms and sounds that accompanied them to convey their meaning. The politics of CND, representative of a general distrust of the older generation of political masters who had dominated British politics since the war (culminating in Harold Macmillan), provided a common starting point.

Poetry in the 60s appeared to be enjoying something of a renaissance with the growth in popularity of public readings, bringing together musicians and poets of the new wave. Three Liverpool poets, Adrian Henri, Roger McGough and Brian Patten became the idols of this movement, along with Adrian Mitchell and Thom Gunn. Poems like Henri's 'Bomb Commercials' linked a way of life dominated by commercialism with the frightening implications of the nuclear arms race. McGough's 'Motorway' similarly identified modern society's rage for communications with the dangerous political direction of the age:

> The politicians,
> (who are buying huge cars with hobnailed wheels
>   the size of merry-go-rounds)
>   have a new plan.
>   They are going to
>   put cobbles
>   in our eyesockets
>   and pebbles
>   in our navels
>   and fill us up
>   with asphalt
>   and lay us
>   side by side
> so that we can take a more active part
>   in the road
>   to destruction.[15]

John Wain, initially identified with The Movement, changed his style dramatically from that of his *New Lines* contributions to social comment in *Weep Before God* (1962). The final poem in that volume, 'A Song About Major Eatherly', was inspired by the fate of the pilot of the plane which dropped the bomb on Nagasaki:

> Good news. It seems he loved them after all.
> His orders were to fry their bones to ash.
> He carried up the bomb and let it fall.
> And then his orders were to take the cash,
>
> A hero's pension. But he let it lie.
> It was in vain to ask him for the cause.
> Simply that if he touched it he would die.
> He fought his own, and not his country's wars.[16]

The central theme of the 60s pop movement was to challenge high culture; its target was the Establishment, and it gestured towards a populist, specifically political style. The subtle use of formal structure gave way to rhythms directly influenced by an emphatic musical beat, or to free verse; the language was frequently colloquial and jokily inventive; the intention was generally to avoid the temptation of taking language too seriously and producing what might sound like 'great' poetry. The result was often to fall into the kind of inverted-pretentiousness trap that not infrequently characterized the lyrics of John Lennon. At the point when its widespread popularity was evidently on the wane, Alvarez sought to explain the reasons for pop poetry's inadequacy:

[15] *The Mersey Sound*, Revised Edition, Penguin Books (1983), p. 99.
[16] John Wain, *Weep Before God*, London: Macmillan (1962), p. 40.

> In its way, this is largely a political project: art is valuable simply as a means of rejecting the square world. So the poet resigns his responsibilities; he becomes less concerned to create a work than to create a public life; what he offers is not poetry but instant protest. Where the pop painter becomes an interior decorator, the pop poet becomes a kind of unacknowledged social worker.
>
> (*Lucie-Smith 1970*, p. 393)

Difficult to assess as this aspect of 60s poetry still is, Alvarez's comments are certainly too dismissive. The popular music scene remains a productive source of potentially interesting and important work, though it continues to operate as a distinct genre, defined by music journalists and fellow-travelling academics, rather than by its proponents.

Mainstream British poetry evolved away from the possibilities offered by the now dated protest rhetoric of poetry written in the 1960s. The growing economic strictures of the 70s and 80s, and England's decline as a major political power since the war has had a significant influence here. By way of contrast, the political consciousness of American poets has arguably fostered a consistently more impressive radical tradition of protest poetry, chiefly because of the effect which 'super-power' status and responsibility tends to have on the cultural self-awareness of a nation.

From the vantage-point of the 1980s, the pop revolution of the 60s can now appear tame, even picturesque, at worst a useful target for contemporary politicians who wish to locate the reason for present moral laxity as far away as possible from their own doorsteps. The protest it articulated, whether in politically unfocused terms of generation-gap rebellion, or on more specifically political issues, was the product of a 'never-had-it-so-good' confidence, when wearing National Health spectacle frames was a coy way of proclaiming yourself wealthy enough to choose not to buy alternatives. The heirs to the iconoclasm of the Liverpool poets are John Bains, John Cooper Clarke, Linton Kwesi Johnson, and others operating on the fringe of the entertainment business. In a period when unemployment stands at a record post-war level and shows no clear sign of falling, when racial tension and social unrest is made manifest with increasing regularity in the form of violent protest and inner-city rioting, and when many of the traditional features of a British 'way of life' are held to be threatened, there is little room left for the good natured banter which characterized so much of the original pop poetry output. The atmosphere has changed to one of aggression, anger and obscenity, a conscious fouling of anything even remotely associated with Establishment status:

> well mi dhu day wok an' mi dhu nite wok
> mi dhu clean wok an' mi dhu dutty wok
> dem seh dat black man is very lazy
> but if y'u si how mi wok y'u woulda sey mi crazy

> Inglan is a bitch
> dere's no escapin it
> Inglan is a bitch
> y'u bettah face up to it[17]

It has fallen to the lot of Scottish, Irish and Welsh poets to provide the most insistent note of political awareness within the mainstream of British poetry from which Bains, Clark and Johnson strategically distance themselves. England is viewed tangentially by the rest of Britain, whose economic and social problems may be seen as visited upon them. For Scotland, Wales and Ireland there exist alternative cultural and linguistic perspectives, and often a more natural sense of relationships both with Europe and the United States. The work of the Welsh poet R.S. Thomas will be considered later. The father figure of twentieth-century Scottish poetry is Hugh MacDiarmid, whose Marxist commitment resulted in his belief, as Edward Lucie-Smith has pointed out, 'that all art must be "social art"' (*Lucie-Smith* p. 297). Since MacDiarmid, Scottish poets have pioneered experimental writing, notably Edwin Morgan and Ian Hamilton Finlay. Though without the extreme political crisis experienced in Ireland over the last twenty years, Scotland's economic and political problems have been sufficient to create an atmosphere not unlike that described by Blake Morrison and Andrew Motion as facing Irish poets:

> The poets have all experienced a sense of 'living in important places' and have been under considerable pressure to 'respond'. They have been brought hard up against questions about the relationship between art and politics, between the private and the public, between conscious 'making' and intuitive 'inspiration'.
>
> (*CBP* p. 16)

Alan Bold is probably the most politically doctrinaire of the Scottish poets, his 'June 1967 at Buchenwald' is an uncompromising statement in bleak free verse of the way the political lessons of the past can be all too easily put to one side with 'our arrogant/Assumption that we are immune as well/As apathetic':

> There is the viciously vicarious in us
> All. The pleasure in chance misfortune
> That lets us patronize or helps to lose
> Our limitations for an instant.
> It is that, that struggle for survival
> I accuse. Let us not forget
> Buchenwald is not a word. Its
> Meaning is defined with every day.
> Everybody gets what he deserves.
> (*Lucie-Smith* p. 323)

[17]Linton Kwesi Johnson, *Inglan is a Bitch*, London: Race Today Publications (1981), p. 27.

In England The Movement effectively claimed the centre ground for poetry. In retrospect Conquest, Davie, Enright and the others were matching their view of what poetry and public taste should be to the political and social model for British society of the late 40s and early 50s with considerable precision. Arguably there never has been, and never can be a resting place of this kind for poetry. Certainly since the evolution of modern industrial Britain (leading now perhaps to a post-industrial era), poetry has repeatedly moved towards the margins; the tendency is essentially that initiated in the first expression of disaffection with a centre ground defined by Classicism in the eighteenth century. As British society since the war has shown increasing signs of fragmentation, and as the political and economic context has changed radically with the demise of a consensus ideal, the course taken by much British poetry away from the idea of 'a certain unity of approach, a new and healthy general standpoint' (*New Lines* p. xiv), has done no more than confirm that British society itself has long since left the Movement's appeal to aesthetic consensus behind. Poetry has evolved as an integral part of society, and increasingly in Britain as this century has progressed, the traditional idea that 'great literature was universal and expressed general truths about human life'[18] has been eroded as notions about universal and general truths governing society have been increasingly difficult to sustain. The function of literary criticism as it evolved after Arnold has steadily had its assumptions eroded by the same pressures. The class divisions of pre-war Britain have clearly not been swept away by the 'people's war' of 1939–45, and new, profoundly disruptive forces have created a continuing atmosphere of crisis and division.

Poets like Ted Hughes, R.S. Thomas (b. 1913) and Geoffrey Hill have all pursued in different ways a theme of spiritual survival in the face of seemingly overwhelming odds. Their work affirms the function of the poet as one who draws us away from cynicism and compromise regardless of the cost. Thomas's poetry confronts the reader with the grim, unrelenting prospect of a depopulated Welsh landscape apparently devoid of hope. Through sheer effort of will, Thomas sustains a grain of optimism for humanity, turning to Shelley as his point of reference for a belief in at least the possibility that there is a future for the life of man stripped to the unsentimental essentials. 'Song at the Year's Turning' begins with the statement, 'Shelley dreamed it. Now the dream decays'; but the implied optimism of the title is borne out in the final lines: 'Winter rots you; who is there to blame?/The new grass shall purge you in its flame.'[19]

A period of intense scientific and technological development, of space

---

[18]Raman Selden, *A Reader's Guide to Contemporary Literary Theory*: Brighton: Harvester (1985) p. 1.
[19]'Song at the Year's Turning' appears in *Selected Poems 1946–68*, London: Hart-Davis (1973), p. 35. The other poems quoted here, 'Cynddylan on a Tractor' and 'Affinity' are not in *Selected Poems*. All three poems are to be found in *Penguin Modern Poets* Vol. I (Lawrence Durrell, Elizabeth Jennings, R.S. Thomas), Penguin Books (1962).

travel and spare-part surgery, is seen by Thomas as having also been one of profound spiritual destitution for humanity, regardless of its relative prosperity. Thomas's poetry is at heart political; the steady disintegration of the identity of Wales ultimately serves as a metaphor for the condition of every reader of his poetry. The image of the Welsh hill farmer, Cynddylan on his new tractor, is one of diminution, even ridicule, not newly acquired strength:

> Ah, you should see Cynddylan on a tractor.
> Gone the old look that yoked him to the soil;
> He's a new man now, part of the machine,
> His nerves of metal and blood oil...

Retreat to cynical despair in the manner of Larkin is dishonesty in Thomas:

> ... Don't be taken in
> By stinking garments or an aimless grin;
> He also is human, and the same small star,
> That lights you homeward, has inflamed his mind
> With the old hunger, born of his kind.
>
> ('Affinity')

In many respects Hughes's *Crow* confronts us with a similarly bleak challenge, while Hill (b. 1931), in an unrepentantly difficult, metaphysical style, looks to religion, history and myth for the light of hope that can burn so dimly for Thomas. In *Mercian Hymns* (1971) past and present collide in a remarkable evocation of the timeless qualities of human experience. The present is rescued by being interwoven with the distant past, figured at times as being literally dug out of the earth, not unlike Heaney's bog people. The ghosts of Offa's time become increasingly real, solid presences as the hymns progress, the trappings of our own time are gradually diminished in significance:

> King of the perennial holly-groves, the riven sandstone: overlord of the M5: architect of the historic rampart and ditch, the citadel at Tamworth, the summer hermitage in Holy Cross: guardian of the Welsh Bridge and the Iron Bridge: contractor to the desirable new estates: saltmaster: moneychanger: commissioner for oaths: martyrologist: the friend of Charlemagne.
>
> 'I liked that,' said Offa, 'sing it again.'[20]

With the publication of the *Collected Poems* in 1985, considerable claims

---

[20]Geoffrey Hill, 'Mercian Hymns' I (1971), in *Collected Poems*, Penguin Books (1985), p. 105.

have been made for Hill's status as a major poet, claims which have inevitably not been allowed to go unchallenged.[21]

Other poets have concentrated on the concept of art itself as redefining reality away from false contemporary perspectives. Charles Tomlinson's contribution has been particularly important in this respect. Generally labelled as a poet influenced primarily by American imagists, he represents a persistent strand of the British tradition which has resisted insularity. His 'Meditation on John Constable' is a difficult but central statement of his position. Complex as the whole poem may be, the final lines are unequivocal:

> ... The artist lies
> For the improvement of truth. Believe him.[22]

A summary of the position of British poetry in the early 1980s is offered by Blake Morrison and Andrew Motion in their Introduction to the *Penguin Book of Contemporary British Poetry*; it is an important document, and the authors see it as a statement to be set alongside the other major post-war manifestos by Conquest and Alvarez. While the terms Romantic and Classical can now no longer be used to carry the weight of significance they continued to retain up to the Second World War, it is fascinating to see the way Morrison and Motion identify the contemporary scene in terms evidently still analogous to the Classical/Romantic duality that began to evolve two centuries ago. Contemporary British poetry, they argue:

> ... represents a radical departure from the empirical mode which was conspicuous ... in British poetry of the 1950s and 60s. The new poetry is often open-ended, reluctant to point the moral of, or conclude too neatly, what it chooses to transcribe. And it reasserts the primacy of the imagination in poetry, having come to see the imagination ... as a potential source of tenderness and renewal.
>
> (*CBP* p. 12)

With the changes that have taken place over the century in mind, we are bound to reflect at this point on the Imagist rejection of Romantic 'slither', on the rediscovery of Romantic spontaneity in the light of the Surrealist reaction to Modernism, and on The Movement's rejection of the Apocalyptics and the domination of the Id. Poetry is now being offered as a medium capable of transcending harmful divisions within society, it is essentially an imaginative transcendance that cannot be purchased at the level of trite political propaganda, nor at the level of common-sense observations made by 'the poet as the-person-next-door' (*CBP* p. 12), dismissive of academicism and sociological jargon. If this seems to suggest a degree of Romantic revival, there are also indications of a revival of Modernism in

---

[21] See 'Geoffrey Hill: refined, furious – and great?', in *TLS* 4 April, 1968, pp. 363–4.
[22] Charles Tomlinson, 'Meditation on John Constable', *Seeing Is Believing* (1960), in *Selected Poems 1951–1974*, London: Oxford University Press (1978), p. 20. Hereafter, *Tomlinson*.

Morrison and Motion's idea of the contemporary poet as now 'the anthropologist or alien invader or remembering exile' (*CBP* p. 12). But what binds these poets together in a 'shift of sensibility' (*CBP* p. 12) sufficient to think in terms of the development of a distinct contemporary school is 'the sense of common purpose: to extend the imaginative franchise' (*CBP* p. 20).

Seamus Heaney is placed at the head of the collection, and other members of the Belfast group are represented. The perpetuation of the sense of dislocation with 'the cultural establishment' (*CBP* p. 17) which Larkin's work emphasized and which became evident in different ways in the 1960s is perpetuated in the anthology by the inclusion of Tony Harrison (b. 1937) and Douglas Dunn (b. 1942). Both are poets who draw frequent attention to their working-class origins, yet both indicate that poetry has in practice separated them from their roots:

> I thought it made me look more 'working class'
> (as if a bit of chequered cloth could bridge that gap!)
> I did a turn in it before the glass.
> My mother said: *It suits you, your dad's cap.*
> (Tony Harrison, 'Turns', *CBP* p. 47)

Equally suggestive of the political edge that is now an established part of contemporary poetry is the work of women writers responding to the sexual politics of feminism. Fleur Adcock's 'Against Coupling' is a wry comment 'in praise of the solitary act':

> I advise you, then, to embrace it without
> encumbrance. No need to set the scene,
> dress up (or undress), make speeches.
> Five minutes of solitude are
> enough – in the bath, or to fill
> that gap between the Sunday papers and lunch.
> (*CBP* p. 93)

Feminist poetry is still inclined to be taken as implying the use of poetry for Feminist polemic. The anthology illustrates how far from the truth that is, particularly in the selection given of Carol Rumens's work. 'Coming Home' is a subtly balanced comment on the generally claustrophobic atmosphere of English suburbia, though the perception of it arises from a specifically female awareness of stereotyping:

> We chug towards our own front door
> anxiously, seeing as if for the first time
> how tight the plot that locks us in,
> how small our parts, how unchosen.
> (*CBP* p. 160)

One particular aspect of post-war life that seems to be a recurring common factor in the work of most contemporary poets is isolation, an isolation that brings with it the recognition of subjectivity in judgement over against a belief in an empiricism made possible by a sense of shared experience. In many respects this emphasizes the importance of Hughes, Tomlinson and R.S. Thomas for the new generation. The poem is itself a 'making', not simply a reflection. In 'How Still The Hawk' (*Tomlinson* p. 14) Charles Tomlinson (b. 1927) shows how we create 'truth' through art. The poem describes a hawk hovering over a wood. We invest that scene with beauty, and are able to do so partly because 'Distance . . . purifies the act/Of all intent'. The hawk is described as 'innocent' while it seeks a victim below. Thus:

> Beauty must lie
> As innocence must harm
> Whose end (sited,
> Held) is naked . . .

The 'end' which is 'sited' and 'Held' by the motionless hawk is of course the bird's unfortunate prey. The artist clothes the nakedness to make it bearable:

> To love
> is to see,
> to let be
> this disparateness
> and to live within
> the unrestricted boundary between.
> ('Face and Image' in *Tomlinson* p. 58)

James Fenton (b. 1949) writes within these boundaries, though unlike Tomlinson he does not necessarily write in order to expound the philosophy of the situation. Craig Raine has employed the device of assuming an alien identity to emphasize a contemporary relativist view of reality in 'A Martian Sends A Postcard Home' (a device that had already been employed by the Scots poet Edwin Morgan in 'From the Domain of Arnheim'). Fenton is prepared to see himself as the alien presence, needing no assumed persona to make the point about the subjectivity of his art; he is continually investigating the complexities of perception, drawing attention to 'the artifice and autonomy of his text' (*CBP* p. 19). This is a particularly contemporary obsession, nowhere more evident than in the current turbulent debate on matters of literary theory. The disparate, fragmentary narrative strands of 'A Staffordshire Murderer' (*CBP* pp. 112–15) creates a haunting poem, its very disjointedness deconstructing our natural search for formal plot and formal 'interpretation'; its resistance to an orthodox period location and moral statement becomes a primary act of meaning for the poem.

In 'A German Requiem' Fenton uses the destructive experience of war as a metaphor for human experience. Given the poet's intellectual approach to his work, and his sense of modern society as best defined by its absences, it is not surprising that we savour something of Eliot in the following lines. The poem does not create a subject here, it is creating a framework within which we may become aware of the spaces, of the words that are not there, of the discontinuities in need of resolution:

> It is not what they built. It is what they knocked down.
> It is not the houses. It is the spaces between the houses.
> It is not the streets that exist. It is the streets that no longer exist.
> It is not your memories which haunt you.
> It is not what you have written down.
> It is what you have forgotten, what you must forget.
> What you must go on forgetting all your life.
> And with any luck oblivion should discover a ritual.
> You will find out that you are not alone in the enterprise . . .
>
> (*CBP* p. 107)

It is in the crucial act of imagination, here implied through the discovery of 'ritual', that the continuities needed if individuals are to survive will be found. Contemporary society, for all its material advances, seems fitted only for destroying imaginative growth. The act of writing in poetic form, consequently, becomes of increasing significance, embodying the faith, in Seamus Heaney's words, 'that artistic process has some kind of absolute validity' (*Preoccupations* p. 99). This is creativity in its most fundamental form, creativity born of a sense of loss as social, cultural and religious forces fail to cohere and sustain the imaginative act. It is therefore not surprising that much recent poetry is concerned to some extent with the experience of bereavement. Douglas Dunn's *Elegies*[23] is only one example of the genre, though it may well prove to be among the most impressive elegaic achievements of the century.

Other examples would include Fenton's 'Requiem', Seamus Heaney's 'Mid-Term Break', and several poems from *Fieldwork*, in particular 'Elegy' where he cites the American poet Robert Lowell as 'the master elegist' in a poem which stresses the positive qualities of the genre:

> you found the child in me
> when you took farewells
> under the full bay tree
> by the gate in Glanmore,

---

[23]Douglas Dunn, *Elegies*, London: Faber & Faber (1985).

> opulent and restorative
> as that lingering summertime,
> the fish-dart of your eyes
> risking, 'I'll pray for you.'
> (*Fieldwork* p. 32)

Several of Tony Harrison's poems are dominated by the memory of his mother and father, and there is also Andrew Motion's 'In The Attic', Karen Gershon's 'In the Jewish Cemetery', Carol Rumens's Larkinesque 'December Walk', Larkin's 'The Explosion', and 'Only a Small Death' and 'Lament for the Patients' by U.A. Fanthorpe.[24]

In these and in many other contemporary poems we begin to see how for the poet living now it has become necessary for the work of art itself to reconstruct a life in the absence of the dead. Poems of specific bereavement metaphorically reveal a theme and a purpose that seems to be increasingly persistent as a part of poetic creativity in the latter years of the twentieth century. The function of poetry is positive, it supplies the means of reconciliation and continuity while at the same time recognizing the difficulties that exist in sustaining the belief that such ideals are possible:

> . . . Black as coal
>   I turn to go
> Out of the graveyard. Headstone shadows merge
>   And blur. I see the spire
> Lift over the corpses. And I sense the flow
> Of death like honey to make all things whole.
> (George MacBeth, 'The Shell' in *Lucie-Smith* pp. 187–8)

---

[24]The poems cited by Motion and Rumens are in *CBP*. Gershon's 'In the Jewish Cemetery' is in *Lucie-Smith*. Larkin's 'The Explosion' is in *High Windows*, Faber & Faber (1974). For Fanthorpe see *Selected Poems*, Penguin Books (1986).

Conclusion

'Must all tradition then be set aside?' (Dryden, *Religio Laici* (1682))

In many respects, to argue that Romanticism has played a formative role in the continuing evolution of British poetry from the late eighteenth century through to the 1980s need not be overly contentious. Precisely how that role is perceived at specific points over the last eighty years of that period, however, may lead to controversy; but if we accept that the inception of the Romantic Movement in this country marks a point at which it had become possible to diagnose a fragmentation within society that was of a genuinely new order, and for which traditional remedies (prescribed in traditional rhetorical forms) seemed no longer relevant, the perpetuation and development of Romanticism in some form is only to be expected. Initially it marked a variety of responses to the consequences of the social and political effects of the Industrial Revolution, informed to a significant degree by the political shock waves created by the French Revolution; latterly, Romanticism has denoted a response to the historical interpretation and analysis of these events, alongside the impact of contemporary scientific and technological changes on our society.

One major symptom of radical changes taking place within society, involving particularly class structure, was the progressive loss of a commonly based set of assumptions about literary form, language and points of reference, and their replacement by diversified and often competing forms. This is best illustrated in the late eighteenth century by the gradual assimilation into literary discourse of the term 'Gothic', implying an alternative if not antagonistic literary model to 'Classicism'. Poetry since 1945 increasingly reflects a divergence and plenitude of linguistic forms which arguably began to be possible when, in the course of the eighteenth century, the monopoly of literary production by a minority with a common cultural identity started to disintegrate with the advent of a diversifying readership, and with the development of the technical means to serve a mass market.

Taking Wordsworth as a major influence on the formative period of the Romantic Movement, we can appreciate that endemic to Romanticism was the wish – to some extent at least – to stem the tide of change within the realm of literature, and to retain among the welter of literatures a primary literature which, if it could no longer address important social issues in the old way, at least preserved a formal quality of high seriousness recognizable as the heir to the seventeenth and early eighteenth-century tradition of major poets producing literary works of major cultural and social standing, and influence. Poetry has never lost, and presumably will never lose, its allegiance to that principle, and as we have seen, consistent reference back to Wordsworth in particular appears as an interesting feature of post-Romantic British poetry. This is not to say, however, that in holding to such a principle, the poet is in consequence committed to the constant reproduction of Wordsworthian form.

Romantic remains, therefore, a useful and relevant term where twentieth-century poetry is being assessed. To what extent, though, can we continue to see Classicism as its foil? In this book, the Classical tradition, often identified primarily with the eighteenth-century Augustan tradition, has been referred to by way of helping to place Modernism within a literary context, while subsequent poets and critics, among them Donald Davie, Geoffrey Grigson and Michael Schmidt, have been represented (primarily through their own statements) as individuals seeking to perpetuate a pre-Romantic sensibility. It is important to suggest, therefore, that while the Romantic Movement may be understood as continuing into our own time as a living tradition, growing and changing as time passes, the Augustan tradition is inescapably now historically located in the past. This does not mean that Augustan ideals may not be preserved and expressed; what we do have to recognize is that the society which could produce and sustain such ideals is gone for good, unless, that is, we were to undergo a revolution of the type that could obliterate the social and political consequences of a period beginning with the American Revolution of 1776, and encompassing the French Revolution, the Industrial Revolution, and the fundamental changes brought about by nineteenth-century legislation relating in particular to education and the franchise.

This is not an argument which concludes that poetry written prior to the late eighteenth century has no longer anything to offer us; it is rather to suggest that poetry written now as neo-Augustan must have a far more dubious claim to our attention than that which appears to belong within a broadly defined Romantic tradition. Indeed, it might well be argued that it has now become impossible to write out of a genuinely Augustan Classical frame of mind. We cannot recapture a social standpoint which no longer exists. The tradition of criticism which – despite differences of detail – links Arnold, Pound, Eliot, Grigson and Leavis through their opposition to Romanticism, is properly understood as a response to twentieth-century society which has sought to use a pre-Romantic stick with which to beat a range of liberal or left-wing views affecting art and society as it has evolved since the nineteenth century. The literary and political base of such criticism, however, is located firmly in the post-Romantic era rather than Augustan England.

Conclusion

The fascination that eighteenth-century poetry continues to have for contemporary poets is nevertheless strong, perhaps the most substantial recent example being George MacBeth's extended sequence of poems called *The Cleaver Garden* (Secker & Warburg, 1986). MacBeth sees himself as having returned to an eighteenth-century mode after searching for the most effective means of constructing a modern poem. Reading *The Cleaver Garden*, however, has led more than one critic to comment that there is at least as much of Tennyson the Romantic in it as of Pope the Augustan satirist.

In the end it would seem that a condition of the post-Augustan poet and critic, regardless of preferences, is to exist in a literary climate where too great an emphasis on historically defined literary models is at best counter-productive. In our own century, it has probably been W.H. Auden as much as any poet who has steered poetry since the Romantic Movement of the early nineteenth century away from this manner of historically compartmentalized thinking, and no post-war poet or school of poets has managed to avoid the consequences of his achievement.

It will certainly become evident that in categorizing various schools of poetry, I have made distinctions in this book that in the end threaten to become too rigid. If they have been useful in creating an initial chart for navigating a route through the century's many poets, then the pigeonholing has been worth while; a more detailed exploration of the area can now begin.

With particular reference to the contemporary period, the proliferation of different and experimental forms of poetry, notably since the 1960s, soon renders the kind of categorization one is inclined to use – based mostly on the pre-war period – Georgian, Modernist, Surrealist, very inadequate. The feeling that contemporary poetry has no clearly defined schools within it in the way it seemed to have up until the war, may be explained by the fact that we are still too close to it to form the judgements necessary. There is, however, another point to make in this respect which suggests an alternative explanation as to why the situation is indeed one where conditions exist that make the post-war period unique in its diversity of poetic voices.

We have now experienced forty years or more free from warfare on the scale of both world wars, longer by far than was known in the first half of the century; this has resulted in a period of cultural evolution where contemporary poetry might be expected to have about it a quality of divergence not previously possible. Twice during the earlier period, there was a sense in which everything 'normal' stopped, and had to some extent to start again.

If the central thread of the argument of this book, the significance of the Romantic Movement for the evolution of twentieth-century poetry, has been in any way successful as a thesis, it should also have emerged that such an approach is a very dangerous game to play. Read's thesis was, as we have seen, that *all* true poets are by definition 'Romantics'; their opposite numbers, the 'Classicists', are not artists in any worthwhile sense of the word.

Equally it must be arguable that the Romantic/Classical dichotomy is eternally present within all artists, as opposed to dividing them into two distinct camps, Romanticism in the end being a literary definition of what is in fact undefinable, contradictory and materially inexplicable in the creative act.

Certainly any recourse to such a body of literature as that produced by the Romantic poets (historically defined) to help define a later body of work is of no use unless we also take into account the very real differences between their own time and ours. Such matters of historical context notwithstanding, it remains important to remember that at all times, the most accessible means of understanding the present has been through interpreting the past; and the modern, no matter how outrageous or distinct it may seem, is always grounded in a response to what has already taken place; discontinuity can only have meaning in juxtaposition to continuity, nonsense – or no sense – can only exist in relation to what has, up to that point, seemed to constitute sense.

Finally, to offer the elegy as a point of conclusion for the previous chapter should after all be recognized as little more than a ploy by which a suitably tidy closure might be achieved for poetry of the 1980s. Any period we care to designate will reveal its elegists. In offering that observation in Chapter 4, I am only doing in critical terms what in creative terms all artists must do (what in the nineteenth century it seemed especially difficult to do), finding the means of drawing tidily into the curb to stop, having first looked into the rear-view mirror. Once stationary, we can use the time to reflect that what we are encouraged to think of as an historically defined Romantic period is, in its most profound sense, still proceeding, and proceeding as much through the composition of poetry as through any art form. In addition, it may begin to be apparent that we cannot expect to understand fully any aspect of our present-day society without recourse to its poetry.

Bibliographies

A. A list, in chronological order, of anthologies which cover the period of this book.

Poems of Faith and Doubt: The Victorian Age, ed. R.L. Brett, London: Edward Arnold (1965).
Georgian Poetry, ed. James Reeves, Penguin Books (1962).
Imagist Poetry, ed. Peter Jones, Penguin Books (1972).
First World War Poetry, ed. Jon Silkin, Penguin Books (1981).
Poetry of the Thirties, ed. Robin Skelton, Penguin Books (1964).
The Chatto Book of Modern Poetry 1915-1955, ed. C. Day Lewis and John Lehmann, London: Chatto & Windus (1968).
New Country: Prose and Poetry by the authors of New Signatures, ed. Michael Roberts, London: Hogarth Press (1933).
The White Horseman: prose and verse of the new apocalypse, ed. J.F. Hendry and Henry Treece, London: Routledge (1941).
Poems of the Second World War, Editor-in-Chief Victor Selwyn, London: Dent (1985).
New Lines, ed. Robert Conquest, London: Macmillan (1967).
The New Poetry, ed. A. Alvarez, Penguin Books (1966).
The Mersey Sound, Penguin Books (1983).
British Poetry Since 1945, ed. Edward Lucie-Smith, Penguin Books (1985).
Poetry 1900-1975, ed. George Macbeth, London: Longmans (1983).
Contemporary British Poetry, ed. Blake Morrison and Andrew Motion, Penguin Books (1982).

B. A list of critical works intended to complement the titles already specified in the text.

Bergonzi B. (ed.) *The Twentieth Century*, London: Sphere Books (1970).
Dodsworth M. *The Survival of Poetry*, London: Faber & Faber (1970).
Dyson A.E. (ed.) *Poetry Criticism and Practise: Developments since the Symbolists*, London: Macmillan (1986).
Halsey A.H. (ed.) *Change in British Society*, London: Oxford University Press (1981).

Harrison T. *Dramatic Verse 1973–85*, Newcastle-upon-Tyne: Bloodaxe (1986).
Johnston D. *Irish Poetry after Joyce*, Mountrath, Portaoise: Dolman Press (1986).
Morrison B. *Seamus Heaney*, London: Methuen (1982).
The Movement, London: Oxford University Press (1980).
Motion A. *Philip Larkin*, London: Methuen (1982).
Perkins D. *A History of Modern Poetry*, London: Harvard University Press (1976).
Rodway A. *A Preface to Auden*, London: Longmans (1984).
Rosenthal and Gall *The Modern Poetic Sequence*, London: Oxford University Press (1983).
Smith S. *W.H. Auden*, Oxford: Basil Blackwell (1985).
Spender S. *The Struggle of the Modern*, London: Methuen (1977).
West T. *Ted Hughes*, London: Methuen (1985).
Young A. *Dada and After: Extremist Modernism and English Literature*, Manchester: Manchester University Press (1981).

Indices

Index of Poets Cited

Including works referred to in the text.
Where poets are referred to solely for their critical work, reference occurs in the General Index.

Adcock, Fleur, 'Against Coupling', 99
Aldington, Richard, 27–8, 29, 35; 'Trench Idyll', 27
Arnold, Matthew, 2–3, 6, 17, 19, 24, 33, 42, 57, 96, 104; *See also* General Index, *Function of Criticism*
Auden W.H., 39–40, 41–55, 74–6; 'O what is that sound', 42; 'Out on the lawn I lie in bed', 43–4; 'A Communist to Others', 49; 'The Summer holds ...', 49–50; 'Easily, my dear, you move ...' & 'September 1st. 1939', 51; 'At the Grave of Henry James', 52–4; 'Vespers', 75–6, 91, 105

Bains, John, 94–5
Barker, George, 45, 61, 62–3, 64; 'Resolution and Dependence', 62–3
Baudelaire, Charles, 37
Beardsley, Aubrey, 6
Belloc, Hilaire, 30
Betjeman, John, 72–3, 79; 'Aldershot Crematorium', 'In Westminster Abbey' & 'Parliament Hill Fields', 72–3
Blake, William, 2–4, 7, 9, 25, 86; *Songs of Experience*, 3–4
Blunden, Edmund, 13, 27
Bold, Alan, 'June 1967 at Buchenwald', 95
Bréton, André, 55
Bridges, Robert, 13, 35

Brooke, Rupert, 13, 27, 32
Browning, Robert, 8; 'Waring', 78
Bunting, Basil, 74
Byron, Lord George Gordon, 48, 57, 77

Calderón, Pedro, 55
Clarke, John Cooper, 94–5
Coleridge, Samuel Taylor, 6, 9–10, 13, 48, 57, 73, 85; *The Rime of the Ancient Mariner*, 10
Crabbe, George, 2

Dante, Alighieri, 25–6, 38; *The Divine Comedy*, 26
Davie, Donald, 96, 104; 'Too Late For Satire', 82
Davies W.H., 13, 35
de la Mare, Walter, 13, 27, 35
Doolittle, Hilda (H.D.), 18–19, 35; 'Oread', 18–19
Douglas, Keith, 'On a Return from Egypt', 66
Dowson, Ernest, 6, 11
Dryden, John, 67, 103
Dunn, Douglas, 99; *Elegies*, 101

Eliot, T.S., 3, 7, 19, 21, 23–8, 37–9, 41–2, 44–8, 54, 57, 61, 76, 101, 104; *The Love Song of J. Alfred Prufrock*, 23–4, 46; *Preludes*, 23; *The Wasteland*, 26, 38–9, 44, 49, 76; *Ash Wednesday*, 46; *Four Quartets*, 46–7, 54; *Gerontion*, 46
Éluard, Paul, 55

Index

Empson, William, 64
Enright, D.J., 96; 'The Interpreters', 96

Fanthorpe, U.A., 102
Fenton, James, 100-1. 'A Staffordshire Murderer', 100; 'A German Requiem', 101
Finlay, Ian Hamilton, 95
Fraser, G.S., 54, 60, 63
Frost, Robert, 13
Fuller, Roy, 'YMCA Writing Room', 64

Gascoygne, David, 55, 60-1, 64-6; 'The Very Image', 55; 'A Wartime Dawn', 65
Gershon, Karen, 'In The Jewish Cemetary', 102
Gilbert, W.S., 6
Goldsmith, Oliver, 2; 'The Deserted Village', 3
Gray, Thomas, 2-3, 5; 'Elegy in a Country Churchyard', 3
Graves, Robert, 12, 37; 'In Broken Images', 61
Gunn, Thom, 81-2, 92; 'Modes of Pleasure', 'Merlin in the Cave' & 'On The Move', 92

Hardy, Thomas, 6-7, 11-13, 18-19, 28, 35; *Wessex Poems*, 11; *The Dynasts*, 11-12; 'Going and Staying', 12
Harrison, Tony, 102; 'Turns', 99
Heaney, Seamus, 35, 86-91, 97, 99, 101-2; *Death of a Naturalist*, 87; 'At A Potato Digging', 87-8; 'The Tollund Man', 'Kinship', 89, 'Casualty', 90-1; 'Elegy', 101-2
Hendry, J.F., 60, 62; 'Europe: 1939', 60
Henri, Adrian, 92
Hill, Geoffrey, 96-8; *Mercian Hymns*, 97
Hobsbaum, Philip, 86-7
Hopkins, G.M., 35, 48, 61, 84, 87
Horace, 1, 75
Housman, A.E., 'A Shropshire Lad', 16
Hughes, Ted, 35, 83-6, 89, 92, 96-7, 100; 'The Horses', *The Hawk in the Rain*, 84; *Crow*, *Wodwo* & 'A Horrible Religious Error', 85

Hulme, T.E., 17-18, 35
Huxley, Aldous, 35, 37, 59, 73

Jennings, Elizabeth, 'In The Night', 80-1
Johnson, Linton Kwesi, 'Inglan is a Bitch', 94-5
Johnson, Lional, 6, 11
Johnson, Samuel, 3
Juvenal, 1

Keats, John, 18, 48, 86-7
Kerouac, Jack, 74
Keyes, Sidney, 'The Bards', 66
Kipling, Rudyard, 14

Laforgue, Jules, 18, 23
Larkin, Philip, 59, 76-81, 83, 85-6, 92, 97, 99, 102; And Yeats and Hardy, 76; 'Days', 76; 'Poetry of Departures', 'Toads', 77; 'Church Going', 78-9; 'The Whitsun Weddings', 79
Lawrence, D.H., 37, 39, 61, 63, 74, 84
Lennon, John, 93
Lewis, C. Day, 4, 44, 65; *The Magnetic Mountain*, 44; 'Watching Post', 65
Lewis, Alun, 66
Lewis, Wyndham, 36
Lowell, Amy, 35
Lowell, Robert, 101
Lucie-Smith, Edward, 86

MacBeth, George, 86; 'The Shell', 102; *The Cleaver Garden*, 105
MacDiarmid, Hugh, 95
MacNiece, Louis, 42, 45
McCaig, Norman, 60
McGough, Roger, 92-3; 'Motorway', 93
Mahon, Derek, 'Rage for Order', 91
Mallarmé, Stéphane, 11, 37
Masefield, John, 13, 27, 35
Milton, John, 1, 76; *Paradise Lost*, 1
Mitchell, Adrian, 92
Monro, Harold, 23
Moore, Nicholas, 60
Moore, Sturge, 6
Morgan, Edwin, 95; 'From the Domain of Arnheim', 100
Motion, Andrew, 'In The Attic', 102;

112

See also Penguin Book of Contemporary British Poetry in General Index
Muldoon, Paul, 'Anseo', 91-2

Newbolt, Henry, 14-16, 33; 'He Fell Among Thieves', 14-16

Ovid, *Metamorphosis*, 44
Owen, Wilfred, 28-35, 49, 84; 'The Show', 28-9; 'The Dead-Beat', 29-30; 'Mental Cases', 30; 'Miners', 30-1

Patten, Brian, 92
Paulin, Tom, 'Under the Eyes', 91
Pitter, Ruth, 71
Pound, Ezra, 21-3, 26, 28, 35-6, 39, 45, 48, 61, 74, 104
Pope, Alexander, 2, 67, 82, 105
Porter, Peter, 86

Raine, Craig, 100
Read, Herbert, 19, 55-9, 76, 105; *Surrealism and the Romantic Principle*, 55-7; *In Defence of Shelley*, 57; *Wordsworth*, 57-8; 'Meditation of a Dying German Officer', 'A World Within A War', 66
Redgrove, Peter, 86
Reed, Henry, 'Lessons of War', 71
Ridler, Anne, 'The Phoenix Answered', 71
Rimbaud, Arthur, 37
Rickword, Edgell, 37
Rosenberg, Isaac, 33-5, 84; 'Break of Day in the Trenches', 33-5
Rumens, Carol, 'Coming Home', 99; 'December Walk', 102

Sackville-West, Vita, 71
Sassoon, Siegfried, 28-35, 66; 'Break of Day', 32-3; 'Suicide in the Trenches', 34
Scott, Tom, 60
Scott, Walter, 13
Scovell, E.J., 71
Shelley, P.B., 2, 6-7, 22, 48, 57, 76, 96; *Prometheus Unbound*, 22
Sitwell, Edith, 35-7, 54, 68-9; 'The Man With The Green Patch', *Façade*, 37; *Three Poems Of The Atomic Age*, 68-9
Southey, Robert, 13
Spender, Stephen, 41, 45
Stevens, Wallace, 74
Swinburne, Charles Algernon, 6

Tasso, 1
Tennyson, Alfred, 7, 25, 105
Thomas, Dylan, 60, 63-5, 84; 'And Death Shall Have No Dominion', 'In Memory of Anne Jones', 63
Thomas, Edward, 13-16, 26, 29; 'The Owl', 14
Thomas, R.S., 95-7, 100; 'Song at the Year's Turning', 96; Cynddylan on a Tractor', 'Affinity', 97
Tomlinson, Charles, 74, 77, 83, 98, 100; 'Meditation on John Constable', 98; 'How Still The Hawk', 'Face and Image', 100
Treece, Henry, 63

Verhaeren, Émile, 18
Virgil, 1

Wain, John, 'A Song About Major Eatherly', 93
Warner, Rex, 4
Warton, Thomas, 3-4, 42; 'Ode, Sent to a Friend', 3-4
Watkins, Vernon, 45, 60
Whitman, Walt, 18
Wilde, Oscar, 6
Williams, William Carlos, 74
Wordsworth, William, 2-10, 13, 18, 22, 25, 39, 43-4, 48, 51, 57, 76, 84-7, 103-4; *Lyrical Ballads*, 3, 5, 8-10, 76; *Home At Grasmere*, 5-6, 51; 'Expostulation and Reply', 'The Tables Turned', 5; *The Prelude*, 10, 22, 57; *The Excursion*, 57; *Resolution and Independence*, 62, 85

Yeats, W.B., 6, 11, 22-6, 28, 39, 86, 88; 'The Rose of the World', 9; 'The Man who Dreamed of Faeryland', 11; *Responsibilities*, 23; 'Easter 1916', *Michael Robartes and the Dancer*, 24

Zukofsky, Louis, 74

General Index

Including abbreviated forms of texts, to show where full reference is to be found in footnotes.

Abrams, 2
Ackroyd, 23
Aeschylus, 2
Aiken, Conrad, 23
Alvarez A., *The New Poetry*, 82-3, 92-4, 98
American Revolution, The, 21, 104
Anarchism, 58
Anglo-Saxon poetry, 84
Apocalyptic poetry, 60-2, 73, 98; *The New Apocalypse, The White Horseman, & The Crown and the Sickle*, 60
Auden, 40
'Auden Group', The, 41, 54-5, 59, 64
Augustanism, 1-16, 42, 82

Ballad form, 12, 16, 29-31
Bardic poetry, 4, 10, 23, 66
British Broadcasting Corporation, 70, 79
Beatty, Arthur, 59
Beatles, The, 92
Betjeman, 72
Bloomsbury Group, The, 36, 54
Boer War, 20
Buddhism, 23

Carcanet Press, 22
CBP, 91
Churchill, Winston, 70
Civil War (English), 26
Civil War (Spanish), 48
Classicism, 1-16, 17, 19, 42, 54, 56, 58, 75, 96, 98, 103-6

Coghill, Neville, 45
Conquest, Robert, *New Lines*, 59-60, 73-4, 80, 96, 98
Conrad, Joseph, *The Secret Agent*, 21
Consonant rhyme, 28
Craig, 8
Criterion, The, 22
Cubism, 36

Dada-ism, 35
Damon, S. Foster, 59
Darbishire, Helen, 59
Darwin, Charles, 20
Decadents, The, 6
Dickens, Charles, 20; *Bleak House*, 20-1, 26; *Hard Times*, 20

Easter Rising (1916), 22
Elegy, The, 3, 101-2, 106
Eliot S.E., 25
Enlightenment, The, 67

Faber Book of Modern Verse (1936), 41
Fascism, 7, 22, 26
Fieldwork, 90
Feminist poetry, 99
First World War, 7, 13, 27-8
First World War poetry, 27-35; compared with Second World War poetry, 65
Forster, E.M., *Howard's End* and liberal humanism, 21
Free verse (*vers libre*), 18-19, 25, 27, 33-4, 66, 68, 74-7, 93, 95

115

Index

French Revolution, The, 2, 5, 10, 48, 103, 104
Freud, Sigmund, 20, 57, 73–4, 82–3; and Auden, 50
Function of Criticism, The (Arnold), 2–3, 96

Galsworthy, John, *The Man of Property, Strife*, 21
General Election of 1945, 70
Georgian poetry, 13–16, 25, 26–8, 31–3, 35, 37, 50, 65, 71–3, 105
Glob, P.V., 88
Goodbye To All That (Graves), 12, 61
Gothic, 2, 9, 103
Grail legend, 38
Grigson, 63
Grigson, Geoffrey, 63, 67, 104; *New Verse*, 54
Group, The, 86, 92

Haiku poetry, 18
Half-rhyme, 90
Havens, R.D., 59
Heaney S.P., 87
Hughes, 84

Iambic metre, 29, 33
Imagination, 3, 98–9
Imagism, 7, 13, 17–20, 26, 28, 33–4, 45, 65, 74, 88, 98
Imperialism, 14–15, 20
Industrial Revolution, The, 20, 104
Irish poetry and 'the troubles', 88–92

Japanese poetry, 18
Jazz, 92
Jones, 17

Kemp, Peter, 61
Keynes, Sir Geoffrey, 59
Kirkham, Michael, 77
Kumar, Krishnan, 70

Leavis, F.R., 45, 57, 104; *New Bearings in English Poetry*, 48–9
Less Deceived, 77
Lewis, C.S., 59
Liberal humanism, 17, 20–1

Liverpool Poets, The, 92
L.S., 45
Lucie-Smith, 64
Lucie-Smith 1970, 85
Lyric poetry, 12

Macmillan, Harold, 92
Marsh, Edward, 13
Martian poetry, 100
Marxism, 20, 50, 95
Mellors, Wilfred, 92
Mendelson, Edward, 39
Metaphysical poetry, 36
Modernism, 1–3, 6–7, 13, 16, 17–40 passim, 71, 73, 104–5
Morrison, Arthur, *The Children of the Jago*, 21
Morrison, Blake, 95, 98–101
Motion, Andrew, 95, 98–101
Movement, The, 59, 63, 73–4, 77–83, 86, 92–3, 96, 98
Murry, John Middleton, 37

Nagasaki, 93
New Bearings, 48
New Country, 41
New Lines, 59
New Poetry, 81
New Signatures, 41
New Verse, see Grigson, Geoffrey
Nihilism, 81–2

Oasis, 64
Ode, *see* Pindaric Ode
Osborne, John, 86

Para-rhyme, 28–9
Parsons, I.M., 35
Pelican Guide VII, 20
Pelican Guide VIII, 70
Penguin Book of Contemporary British Verse, 'Introduction', 95, 98–9
Peschmann, Herman, 71
Picasso, Pablo, 36
Pindaric Ode, 18, 33
Pinto, 1
Plato, 2
Poetry Nation (*PN Review*), 67
Pop poetry, 92–4

Index

'Preface' to *Lyrical Ballads* (Wordsworth), 3, 5, 8–9, 76
Preoccupations, 86
Pre-Raphaelite Movement, 7
Punch Magazine, 30

Raine, Kathleen, 59
Renaissance, The, 17, 23, 56
Rhymers' Club, The, 11
Richards, I.A., 58
Riding, Laura, 37
Roberts, Michael, 41
Robespierre, Maximilien, 10
Romanticism, 1–16, 17, 19, 73–4, 76, 80–3, 85, 98, 103–6; and liberal humanism, 20–2, 24–5; and post-Modernist poetry, 42–5; and post-1930s neo-Romanticism, 55–69

Sassoon, 32
Sayers, Dorothy, 59
Schmidt, Michael, 12, 22–3, 38, 61, 67–8, 81, 82, 85, 104
Schmidt, 12
Second World War, 7, 55, 96, 98, 105
Second World War poetry, 60–9
Seeley, Sir John, *The Expansion of England in the Eighteenth Century*, 20
Selincourt, Ernest de, and Wordsworth's *Prelude*, 57, 59
Shamanism, 84
Shelley, 57
Shires, 54
Silkin, 14
Sitwell, 37
Skelton, 44
Smith, 39
'Stream of consciousness', 36
Surrealism, 35–6, 55–69, 73, 98, 105
Surrealism, 56

'Swinging sixties', The, 92
Syllabic metre, 75
Symbolism, 8–11, 18, 23, 25, 88
Symbolism, 7
Symons, Arthur, *The Symbolist Movement in Literature*, 11, 23

Tacitus, 89
The Making of the Reader (Trotter), 67
The Making of Dreams (Graves), 61
The Voice of Poetry 1930-50 (Peschmann), 71
The White Goddess (Graves), 61
Thurley, 42
Thwaite, Anthony, 88
Tiresias, 44, 49
Tomlinson, 98
Tradition and the Individual Talent (Eliot), 25
Trotter, 22

Upanishads, The, 39

Vers libre, *see* Free verse
Vorticism, 35–6

Walton, William, 37
Waugh, Evelyn, *Vile Bodies*, 37
Wells, H.G., *The History of Mr Polly*, 21
Wesker, Arnold, 86
Wheels, 35
White Horseman, 60
Whitsun Weddings, 76
Williams, Charles, 59, 61
Williams, John, 10n
Williams, Raymond, 17
Wilson, Mona, 59
Woolf, Virginia, 36, 39
Wordsworth, 58
Workers' Educational Association, 71